TOOLS of the TRADE
Methods of Evangelism

Melinda Poitras

A Global Association of Theological Studies Publication

Unless otherwise noted, all Scripture quotations are from the King James Version of the Holy Bible, which is in public domain.

Scripture quotations marked ESV are from The ESV® Bible (The Holy Bible, English Standard Version®). ESV® Text Edition: 2016. Copyright © 2001 by Crossway, a publishing ministry of Good News Publishers. The ESV® text has been reproduced in cooperation with and by permission of Good News Publishers. Unauthorized reproduction of this publication is prohibited. All rights reserved.

Scripture quotations marked NASB are from the NEW AMERICAN STANDARD BIBLE®, Copyright © 1960,1962,1963,1968,1971,1972,1973,1975,1977,1995 by The Lockman Foundation. Used by permission.

Scripture quotations marked NIV are from THE HOLY BIBLE, NEW INTERNATIONAL VERSION®, NIV® Copyright © 1973, 1978, 1984, 2011 by Biblica, Inc.® Used by permission. All rights reserved worldwide.

Scripture quotations marked NLT are taken from the Holy Bible, New Living Translation, copyright © 1996, 2004, 2015 by Tyndale House Foundation. Used by permission of Tyndale House Publishers, Inc., Carol Stream, Illinois 60188. All rights reserved.

Scripture quotations marked NLV are taken from the New Life Version, copyright © 1969 and 2003. Used by permission of Barbour Publishing, Inc., Uhrichsville, Ohio 44683. All rights reserved.

Copyright 2020
United Pentecostal Church International

Library of Congress Cataloging-in-Publication Data

Names: Poitras, Melinda, author.
Title: Tools of the trade : methods of evangelism / by Melinda Poitras.
Description: Weldon Spring : Global Association of Theological Studies, 2020. | Summary: "This book summarizes various methods of effectively evangelizing a community with the gospel"-- Provided by publisher.
Identifiers: LCCN 2020004316 | ISBN 9780757761225 (paperback)
Subjects: LCSH: Evangelistic work--Study and teaching. | Evangelistic work--Methodology.
Classification: LCC BV3796 .P65 2020 | DDC 269'.2--dc23
LC record available at https://lccn.loc.gov/2020004316

Global Missions gratefully acknowledges
The Sanctuary
Hazelwood, Missouri
Tim Dugas, Scott Graham, and Mitchell Bland, pastors
and its donation of $5000 to fund the production and translation of
Tools of the Trade: Methods of Evangelism
by Melinda Poitras

Table of Contents

1. Evangelism — 7
2. Friendship — 15
3. World Wide Web — 23
4. Product Placement — 31
5. Prayer-Centric Evangelism — 39
6. A Lifestyle of Holiness — 47
7. Radio Evangelism — 55
8. Hospitality — 63
9. Humanitarian Aid — 71
10. Home Bible Studies — 79
11. Knowing the Word — 87
12. Community Outreach — 95
13. Financial Giving — 103
14. The Evangelist — 111
15. Evangelistic Sermons — 119
16. Prison Ministry — 129
17. Reaching the Elderly — 137
18. Door Knocking — 145
19. Cell Groups — 153

Lesson 1

Evangelism

Project Blueprints

After this lesson, students should be able to

- Define *evangelism*
- Understand the scriptural mandate for evangelism
- Know six benefits of evangelism as stated by Brian Parks
- Accept personal responsibility for evangelism

In the Toolbox

Evangelism: the spreading of the Christian gospel by public preaching or personal witness (Merriam-Webster Dictionary).

In His Word

For if I do this thing willingly, I have a reward: but if against my will, a dispensation of the gospel is committed unto me. What is my reward then? Verily that, when I preach the gospel, I may make the gospel of Christ without charge, that I abuse not my power in the gospel. For though I be free from all men, yet have I made myself servant unto all, that I might gain the more. And unto the Jews I became as a Jew, that I might gain the Jews; to them that are under the law, as under the law, that I might gain them that are under the law; to them that are without law, as without law, (being not without law to God, but under the law to Christ,) that I might gain them that are without law. To the weak became I as weak, that I might gain the weak: I am made all things to all men, that I might by all means save some. (I Corinthians 9:17–22)

In Their Shoes

The moment came when Sadie had had enough. The extra pounds she had gained during her pregnancies were causing too many extra problems. Her feet were swelling. Her joints were aching. She was often tired and short of breath. Energy and self-esteem were at an all-time low. Stress and strain were at an all-time high. Nothing in her life was untouched by the weight gain. Her marriage, her friendships, her precious children—everyone was affected by the extra weight she carried. The excess pounds did more than settle on her hips; they sat heavy on her heart, weighing down her mind. Something had to give. Something had to change. So Sadie made up her mind to drastically change her eating habits.

She would shed the weight she so desperately needed to lose, starting that very moment. From that moment on, she would eat only vegetables. Sadie made the decision, and she stuck to it. Veggies for breakfast, lunch, and dinner, all day long, every single day. Her diet consisted entirely of vegetables from the moment she made the decision, and sure enough, the pounds started to fall off.

With the benefit of the weight loss, however, came the weight of other issues. She had even less energy and patience with her family than before. She was tired and testy all the time due to intense headaches and dizziness. Finally, at the insistence of her husband, she visited her doctor. It was then that she learned the source of her health problems was actually the "healthy" diet she had been on.

The doctor informed her that vegetables alone do not contain all the nutrients needed to maintain a healthy, balanced diet, or to take care of her body. The high fiber content in vegetables leads to an unsettled digestive system. Lack of protein, a substance not found in vegetables, leads quickly to a weakened immune system and muscles. Her skin, hair, hormone levels, bones, and blood were all affected by the lack of protein in her diet.

Sadie's doctor showed her something called a "food pyramid" (a diagram of all the different food groups and categories, as well as how much she should be eating from each) and instructed her to open up her food intake to all manner of foods she had not been eating, explaining that a well-balanced diet requires many different types of food—not just vegetables, no matter how good they are for you. All food provides sustenance, but different types of food supply different types of needs.

In Our Hands

The body of Christ is just like a human body. It is made up of different parts that perform different functions. It is our job as believers to seek and save the lost just as Jesus came to do, providing them with the nourishment their souls so desperately need. We offer the Bread of Life (Jesus) and the only sustaining hope this world needs (salvation) to those we cross paths with along the way. This is called evangelism. The necessity of evangelism is undeniable. After all, the whole purpose of Christ on the earth was to reach others, and He left the full weight of that task with His disciples when He ascended into Heaven.

> Then Jesus came to them and said, "All authority in heaven and on earth has been given to me. Therefore go and make disciples of all nations, baptizing them in the name of the Father and of the Son and of the Holy Spirt, and teaching them to obey everything I have commanded you. And surely I am with you always, to the very end of the age." (Matthew 28:18-20, NIV)

Brian Parks published an excellent article on his blog "9Marks" that emphasizes the importance of evangelism for every believer. In this article he lists six benefits of evangelism:

1. Evangelism helps keep the gospel central in our lives and churches.

Just like flour is the main ingredient in bread, the gospel is the main ingredient of the church. The gospel makes the church, is the chief message of it, and is the fuel by which the fire of our faith is kindled. It is up to us to do everything we can to keep the gospel at the center and forefront of everything else we do. Since so many things come against us, trying to stamp out the fire of our faith and distract us from our purpose in Christ, we need to be in the perpetual practice of sharing God's message with those around us. When it becomes all we talk and think about as we go about our days, the benefits work both ways. Prioritizing the gospel compels us to evangelize, and evangelism compels us to prioritize the gospel.

> One way we preserve the gospel is by working hard to pass it on to others. — D. A. Carson
>
> Evangelism helps us maintain the gospel message as the engine of a growing life in Christ. — Brian Parks

2. **Evangelism deepens our understanding of the most fundamental truths of Scripture.**

You cannot have a conversation about soccer unless you know something about it. The more you know about the game, who plays it, what the prominent teams are, what penalty cards mean, the way the rules work, and so forth, the greater your ability to talk about it with someone else.

Evangelism also works that way. In order to explain the gospel to someone else, we must first understand it for ourselves. If we are constantly discussing God's Word and way with others, our understanding of it will deepen due to dwelling on its precepts and promises. We grow in experience as we communicate the same time-tested biblical truths in new ways to different people over time. We may know the fundamental truths of Scripture, but do we know them well enough to communicate them to others in a clear and concise fashion?

3. **Properly motivated evangelism grows our love for God and our neighbor.**

We are called to love others as Christ loved us, thinking of them and caring for them even more than we care for ourselves. A tell-tale sign of this is concern. When something goes wrong in my own life, I am immediately spurred into action. I care quite deeply about the things that affect my own personal time, my family, my relationships, and my bank account. I am concerned because I am affected. The ultimate goal is to care for others just as much as we care for ourselves. To feel their pain, understand their hurt, and relate to the things that are going on in their lives. One of the best ways to cultivate concern for others is to spend time with them. The more our own personal growth and success is tied to others, the more concern we will have for them. In this way, sharing the gospel of Christ enables us to better understand others as well as grow our love for them through shared time and experience.

4. **Evangelism prompts unexpected questions and objections from non-Christians.**

When you take time to share Christ with others, people take notice. Before long you realize you not only are reaching the person you set out to present the gospel of Christ to, but everyone around them as well: the people who observe your interactions with each other, the server who waits on your Bible study table, the family and friends of the person you are witnessing to, and their entire sphere of influence. Hundreds of people might potentially be influenced by your sharing the gospel with one person. Among those people will be those who object to what you are saying or have difficult questions about it. The more opposition you deal with, the more experience you gain in your Christian faith. You will learn to stand against opposition and answer questions with Scripture and with confidence.

5. Evangelism protects us from mistakenly assuming that those around us are saved.

Children in grade school are often asked to do an experiment wherein they pick one color and for the span of a week, look for that color in the world around them. Everywhere they go their eyes search for that one color until, by the end of the week, they are automatically seeing it everywhere they go. If they pick the color purple, suddenly they find themselves living in a predominantly purple world. The planet has no more purple than it had last week, but they have trained their eyes to see it by focusing on it so much that now it appears that the color purple is everywhere.

Evangelism works just like that. The more we focus on the lost and dying world around us, the more we seek opportunities to witness and become more like Him, the more we will notice opportunities to share our faith and the people we need to share that faith with.

6. Evangelism increases the likelihood of being persecuted for the gospel, which leads to our growth.

Persecution is not something we seek out as believers, nor should we. However, the Lord warned us that we might be rejected or misunderstood for His namesake. When we are silent, never taking a stand for what we believe in or "rocking the boat" of the world around us, then few people take issue with us. "Everyone likes a team player." But standing up for the gospel of Christ might bring unwanted attention or persecution our way. Even this works for good in our lives. Even this is a benefit, because standing strong under persecution brings about personal growth.

The necessary and vital practice of evangelism brings about many benefits in our lives and in the lives of those we are called to be a witness to. I began this section of the lesson by stating that evangelism is like the food we hand out to the hurting and hungry body of Christ. Remember Sadie and the vegetables from the "In Their Shoes" segment? Sadie was working hard to accomplish her health goals for the good of her body, but she was attempting to accomplish them in only one way. She was feeding her body only some of the nutrients it desperately needed.

Evangelism can be much like that. We have the Word of God that people need to receive into their lives, but we offer it to them through only one method, over and over again, using only one way. *Numerous* ways abound to serve the bread of Christ. *Countless* ways enable us to share His truth with others in the world around us. We don't just evangelize through one method alone; we recognize different people receive truth in different ways and seek to maximize this message through as many methods as possible. We serve more than vegetables, in a sense, but an entire food pyramid of the gospel. This course is designed to define various methods of evangelism and encourage students to spread the gospel of Jesus to as many people, in as many different ways and places as possible.

> This course is designed to define various methods of evangelism and encourage students to spread the gospel of Jesus to as many people, in as many different ways and places as possible.

In the Workshop

Hold a sword drill with your students. (A "sword drill" is a competition to see who can look up the most verses of Scripture the fastest.) Look up the following verses and discuss how they relate to the lesson:

Colossians 1:5–6	I Corinthians 15:1–3	Philippians 1:6
Philemon 6	Mark 12:28–31	John 15:18–20
Romans 8:5–8	Mark 4:2–8	Romans 5:3–5
II Timothy 1:8	Romans 8:17	Acts 5:41

Final Inspection

1. List five scriptural references mandating evangelism.
   A. _____
   B. _____
   C. _____
   D. _____
   E. _____

2. Do you think likening evangelism to the food pyramid is a good analogy? Why or why not?
   _____
   _____
   _____

3. Summarize Brian Parks's six benefits of evangelism.
    A. _____
    B. _____
    C. _____
    D. _____
    E. _____
    F. _____

4. Write a 500-word essay defending or contradicting Brian Parks's statement: Evangelism helps us maintain the gospel message as the engine of a growing life in Christ.

5. Are you personally committed to evangelism? If no, why not? If yes, what is your present involvement?

_____
_____
_____
_____
_____
_____

Lesson 2

Friendship

Project Blueprints

After this lesson, students should be able to

- Define *friendship*
- Give biblical examples of friendship
- Know what the Bible says about friendship
- Commit to making a new friend
- Understand the concept of "Friendship Evangelism"

In the Toolbox

Friendship: the state of being friends; the quality or state of being friendly (Merriam-Webster Dictionary).

In His Word

> And they continued stedfastly in the apostles' doctrine and fellowship, and in breaking of bread, and in prayers. And fear came upon every soul: and many wonders and signs were done by the apostles. And all that believed were together, and had all things common; and sold their possessions and goods, and parted them to all men, as every man had need. And they, continuing daily with one accord in the temple, and breaking bread from house to house, did eat their meat with gladness and singleness of heart, praising God, and having favour with all the people. And the Lord added to the church daily such as should be saved. (Acts 2:42–47)

In Their Shoes

Peter never forgot the time David invited him to Sunday school. David was the cool kid at their local elementary school. Everyone wanted to be like him and be around him. He had never spoken to Peter before, but one day he walked up to him in the cafeteria and called him by name.

Prior to that moment, Peter had no inkling that David even knew his name. David asked Peter if he would like to hang out with him sometime. When Peter responded that he would (who wouldn't want to hang out with David?) David invited him to go with him to church that Sunday. They arranged a time and place to meet (where a bus would be picking kids up) and parted ways. The rest of the week Peter was so excited! He didn't have many friends at the school, and now the most popular kid in his class had invited him to hang out.

The night before Sunday he barely slept a wink and was up early racing to the meeting place in anticipation. When the bus arrived, he boarded and said hi to David. David smiled and waved, before continuing his conversation with the boy he was already sitting beside. Peter found a seat on the bus and told himself David would pay attention to him when they reached their destination. That never happened. Peter was herded into the church with the rest of the kids. While the teacher was wonderful and friendly and they had fun crafts and delicious snacks, David did little to acknowledge Peter the rest of the morning.

At the end of the lesson, the teacher called David up to the front of the class and offered him a prize for bringing the most people to Sunday school. That was the moment Peter realized that David didn't care much for him at all, but was bringing him to Sunday school not as a friend whose soul was important, but as a body to boost his numbers on the chart. Peter pledged to himself that he would never darken the doors of another church, knowing that all who invited him were only interested in getting him to buy into their religion in order to make themselves look and feel better. Peter had real problems at home and in his life, and he had found no real friend in David or within the church.

The years passed, but that incident stayed fresh in Peter's mind even when he began to grow close to a girl he worked with named Carol. Everyone who met Carol knew she was a Christian, which made Peter leery of her from the very start. However, it was hard to keep his distance from someone like Carol. Her infectious laughter, dedicated work ethic, and caring spirit were a draw to everyone who met her. Carol asked Peter questions about his life, and actually listened to the answers. Carol knew the names of his family members and supported his deepest dreams. The moment Carol approached Peter and asked if he was free on a

Sunday, afternoon Peter winced and braced himself. Here it was, finally the big pitch to boost church attendance.

To his surprise, Carol didn't invite him to church at all. She invited him to Sunday dinner with herself and her family. Peter said yes. Eventually, when Carol did invite Peter to church, she had already proven her genuine care and concern for him, as well as the value she placed on their friendship. Because of this, the boy who had sworn he would never visit another church with another Christian, became a man that Carol led to Christ.

In Our Hands

Friendship evangelism is often looked down upon, even in Christian circles. There are various reasons for this.

1. The idea that you must be friends with someone, living your life next to them and letting your character speak for itself, often negates the obligation to witness.

This means some people feel that communicating the gospel or inviting people to church is wrong, and we should tiptoe gingerly around others, allowing the light of the Holy Spirit to shine through us, but never actually saying anything to them. The idea of "friendship evangelism" as an experience with Christianity by association only is faulty. We are called to communicate the gospel to others, and it is our obligation to tell them the truth about Jesus Christ and the light and life He offers. If we do not tell them, who will?

2. "Friendship Evangelism" is often so much about evangelism that it fails to be an actual friendship at all.

Just like Peter experienced with David, people are sometimes "befriended" as the fulfillment of a clear agenda. Instead of sharing real relationship with someone, people show themselves to be friendly with adding numbers to their community church as the bottom line. This is less genuine care for souls and more a need to satisfy their own agenda. Not only is that not true evangelism, it's not true friendship either.

Problems come into play when friendship is viewed as a means to the end of evangelism, but friendship itself is, and always will be, an important aspect of the kingdom of God. Scripture has much to say about the benefits and necessity of friendship in general:

> Two are better than one, because they have a good return for their labor: if either of them falls down, one can help the other up. But pity anyone who falls and has no one to help them up. . . . Though one may be overpowered, two can defend themselves. A cord of three strands is not quickly broken. (Ecclesiastes 4:9-12, NIV)

> Not forsaking the assembling of ourselves together, as the manner of some is; but exhorting one another: and so much the more, as ye see the day approaching. (Hebrews 10:25)

> Better is open rebuke than hidden love. Wounds from a friend can be trusted, but an enemy multiplies kisses. (Proverbs 27:5-6, NIV)

> A friend loves at all times, and a brother is born for a time of adversity. (Proverbs 17:17, NIV)

> As iron sharpens iron, so one person sharpens another. (Proverbs 27:17, NIV)

> My intercessor is my friend as my eyes pour out tears to God; on behalf of a man he pleads with God as one pleads for a friend. (Job 16:20-21, NIV)

Scripture also offers many examples of relational witnessing, living your life in such a way that those around you will ask questions, and being ready with an answer when they do:

> But sanctify Christ as Lord in your hearts, always being ready to make a defense to everyone who asks you to give an account for the hope that is in you, yet with gentleness and reverence. (I Peter 3:15, NASB)

> Let your light shine before men in such a way that they may see your good works, and glorify your Father who is in heaven. (Matthew 5:16, NASB)

People had some things to say about Jesus Himself in this area. While He preached the gospel clearly and without apology, He also took the time to forge relationships with people. He chose friends that others said He didn't need, but who clearly needed Him:

> The Son of Man came eating and drinking, and you say, "Here is a glutton and a drunkard, a friend of tax collectors and sinners." (Luke 7:34, NIV)

Paul also mentioned the friendship and fellowship he shared with the people of Thessalonica:

> For you yourselves know, brethren, that our coming to you was not in vain, but after we had already suffered and been mistreated in Philippi, as you know, we had the boldness in our God to speak to you the gospel of God amid much opposition. For our exhortation does not come from error or impurity or by way of deceit; but just as we have been approved by God to be entrusted with the gospel, so we speak, not as pleasing men, but God who examines our hearts. For we never came with flattering speech, as you know, nor with a pretext for greed—God is witness—nor did we seek glory from men, either from you or from others, even though as apostles of Christ we might have asserted our authority. But we proved to be gentle among you, as a nursing mother tenderly cares for her own children. Having so fond an affection for you, we were well-pleased to impart to you not only the gospel of God but also our own lives, because you had become very dear to us. For you recall, brethren, our labor and hardship, how working night and say so as not to be a burden to any of you, we proclaimed to you the gospel of God. You are witnesses, and so is God, how devoutly and uprightly and blamelessly we behaved toward you believers; just as you know how we were exhorting and encouraging and imploring each one of you as a father would his own children, so that you would walk in a manner worthy of the God who calls you into His own kingdom and glory. (I Thessalonians 2:1–12, NASB)

These are not the only biblical examples of the importance of relationship in evangelism. Chris Walker provides this list of instances of biblical friendship evangelism encounters on his blog "Evangelism Coach":

- Andrew brought his brother Peter to Jesus (John 1:42–44)
- Philip brought his friend Nathanael (John 1:40-51).
- The Samaritan woman told her whole town about her encounter with Jesus (John 4:28–42).
- The exorcised man from the Gerasenes went home and told his friends how much Jesus had done for him (Mark 5:19–20).
- Matthew invited his friends to a dinner party where they could meet Jesus (Matthew 9:10–13).

- Zaccheus invited many of his friends to a dinner party (Luke 19).
- Jesus was accused of eating with sinners and tax collectors (a relational experience).
- Peter spoke to Cornelius, but the whole household got baptized. Cornelius had brought them (Acts 10:24).
- Paul spent nearly two years talking faith with Felix. At the end of Acts 23, the apostle Paul was sent to Felix, the governor. Felix had Paul guarded in Herod's palace (Acts 23:35) until he had the chance to hear Paul himself (Acts 24). After the hearing, Felix gave Paul some freedom and permitted his friends to take care of his needs (24:23). Felix still got to hear of Jesus and the implication of being a disciple of Christ. These faith-sharing conversations went on for the next two years (verse 27).

The Bible is filled with examples of friendship and relationship being an amazing tool for leading others to Christ and for strengthening their relationship with Him. Even in the Book of Acts, as the verses at the beginning of this lesson state, the church grew because believers met with the people of their communities, breaking bread together in their homes. Building strong friendships and sharing your beliefs is a solid way to strengthen and grow the kingdom of God.

In the Workshop

The Bible is full of examples of great friendships (David and Jonathan, Moses and Aaron, Mary and Elisabeth, and Paul and Aquila and Priscilla). Choose one friendship in the Bible and read and research about it, answering the following questions:

- What made this friendship special?
- What characteristics were displayed in this relationship?
- How can I display those characteristics in my own friendships, making me a better witness to my friends?

Final Inspection

1. In your own words, define *friendship*.

_____

_____

_____

_____

2. List five sets of biblical friends not listed in the lesson.
   A. _____
   B. _____
   C. _____
   D. _____
   E. _____

3. Think of your best friend. What qualities and characteristics make him or her your friend?

   _____
   _____
   _____
   _____

4. What qualities make you a good friend?

   _____
   _____
   _____
   _____

5. What is the difference between an acquaintance and a friend?

   _____
   _____
   _____
   _____

Personal Study Notes

Lesson 3

The World Wide Web

Project Blueprints

After this lesson, students should be able to

- Understand the concept of the internet
- Realize the internet's potential for evangelism
- Choose a medium of choice for personal evangelism involvement using the internet
- Know what content is needed in a church's website

In the Toolbox

Internet: A global computer network providing a variety of information and communication facilities, consisting of interconnected networks using standardized communication protocols.

In His Word

"My name will be great among the nations, from where the sun rises to where it sets. In every place incense and pure offerings will be brought to me, because my name will be great among the nations," says the LORD Almighty. (Malachi 1:11, NIV)

And so I will show my greatness and my holiness, and I will make myself known in the sight of many nations. Then they will know that I am the LORD. (Ezekiel 38:23, NIV)

In Their Shoes

John had been "surfing" the internet for hours. He had always found that term "surfing" to be humorous. It meant clicking from site to site, following the wave of the internet wherever it took him, so it was oddly appropriate, as that is what he had been doing since three in the afternoon. He'd been at it so long that the first signs of dusk were creeping into the evening sky.

He loved music and had been watching video after video. People, he had noticed, were in the habit of making things they called "covers," meaning that someone no one knew would take a popular song and record themselves singing it in their own way. He loved to watch these "covers" as music was a great part of his passion. He knew he should disengage from the endless feed of information and noise in order to actually accomplish some of the work he needed to complete, so he promised himself the next video would be the last.

He clicked on a link and the video began to play, flooding his room with the most angelic sound. He had been experiencing the voices of people with enormous talent all afternoon, but this was different. It was a clip of two girls singing while sitting in the stairwell of some building, which made for the greatest acoustics possible. They were singing a song about Jesus, and there was something different about it, about them, about the whole video. Sure, they were wearing skirts and they had long, uncut hair, but that was not the only thing unusual about them. Their song made him feel like nothing ever had before, and the words they were singing struck a chord deep within him.

As they sang about their love for their God, John encountered God's love for him as the sweetest Spirit filled the room. He clicked on song after song of theirs, the anointing reaching through the internet and touching his heart during each one. He followed the internet trail until he found out that these girls were part of the United Pentecostal Church. He kept researching until he discovered what that church believed, and where he could find one near him. He never did get much accomplished in the way of work the rest of that night, but he did manage to attain eternal salvation.

In Our Hands

According to worldometers.info/world-population, the world's population at 11:49 AM, November 25, 2019, was 7,746,365,805. Of that number, 3,731,973,423 are internet users. This means that about 49 percent of the world's population has access to the internet. If 49 percent of the population has access to the internet, then with the mere click of a mouse, we have access to them as well.

Malachi said God's name would be great among the nations, from where the sun rises to where it sets. (See Malachi 1:11.) Now, using the internet, that beautiful prophecy can be fulfilled with more ease than ever. In fact, Peter Guirguis provides five reasons he feels internet evangelism will be the next big thing:

- Technology has become extremely affordable.
- Internet evangelism has the potential to reach millions of people.
- It's cheap.
- People love to share.
- Non-Christians are searching for God.

Point number five is perhaps the most poignant and powerful. Non-Christians are literally "searching" for God by typing His name into search engines. No one is there to judge them or make them feel pressured when they are surfing the internet, and they are able to google the answers to any question that pops into their mind without the bother or strain of interacting with a human being. CBN.com contributing writer Craig von Buseck states that religion is one of the most popular subjects popping up in web searches worldwide, second only to porn. "Religion used to be number one," he says, "now pornography is. But God is number two and He is very well represented online."

Many examples of the success of internet evangelism exist. David Palmer of Christian Netcast.com shares this one:

> There was a lady a few years ago, she was surfing the Internet looking for ways to kill herself. She was contemplating suicide, and she stumbled across a broadcast. It was actually a live church broadcast, and at the very moment that she got to it, the preacher said, "Someone right now, you're thinking that your life is just not worth it, but you need to know God loves you." That woman fell on her knees at her computer and accepted the Lord.

Now, we preach the full plan of salvation as found in Acts 2:38, but countless instances abound where people have received the gift of the Holy Ghost alone in their bedrooms, and they later sought out someone to baptize them. The Lord is drawing hearts to Him every way possible, and He is willing and able to use us and the internet to aid Him in this endeavor. You can utilize the internet to share your love for Christ in many different ways, with different methods and media:

- **Instagram** is the name of an online, photo-sharing, social web service that lets you share your life with friends through a series of pictures captured with a mobile device.

- **Facebook** is a popular, free, social networking website that allows registered users to create profiles, upload photos and video, send messages, and keep in touch with friends, family, and colleagues. The site, which is available in thirty-seven different languages, includes public features such as:

    o Marketplace—allows members to post, read, and respond to classified ads.
    o Groups—allows members who have common interests to find each other and interact.
    o Events—allows members to publicize an event, invite guests, and track who plans to attend.
    o Pages—allows members to create and promote a public page built around a specific topic.
    o Present technology—allows members to see which contacts are online and chat. (Information provided by whatis.com)

- **Snapchat** is a mobile messaging service from Snap Inc. that sends a photo or video to someone that lasts only up to ten seconds before it disappears. During that time, the recipient can take a screen shot, and the sender is notified that it was taken.

- **YouTube** is a video-sharing service that allows users to watch videos posted by other users and upload videos of their own. The service was started as an independent website in 2005 and was acquired by Google in 2006. Videos that have been uploaded to YouTube may appear on the YouTube website and can also be posted on other websites, though the files are hosted on the YouTube server.

    The slogan of the YouTube website is "Broadcast Yourself." This implies the YouTube service is designed primarily for ordinary people who want to publish videos they have created. While several companies and organizations also use YouTube to promote their business, the vast majority of YouTube videos are created and uploaded by amateurs.

    YouTube videos are posted by people from all over the world, from all types of backgrounds. Therefore, there is a wide range of videos available on YouTube. Some examples include amateur films, homemade music videos, sports bloopers, and other funny events caught on video. People also use YouTube to post instructional videos, such as step-by-step computer help, do-it-yourself guides, and other how-to videos.

    While YouTube can serve as a business platform, most people simply visit YouTube for fun. Since so many people carry digital cameras or cell phones with video recording capability, more events are now captured on video than ever before. While this has created an abundant collection of entertaining videos, it also means that people should be aware that whatever they do in public might be caught on video. And if something is recorded on video, it just might end up on YouTube for the whole world to see. (Information provided by techterms.com)

- A **blog** is a regularly updated website or web page, typically run by an individual or small group, that is written in an informal or conversational style.

- A **podcast** is a digital audio file made available on the internet for downloading to a computer or mobile device, typically available as a series, new installments of which can be received by subscribers only. (Definitions, unless otherwise noted, provided by dictionary.com)

While there is tremendous potential for creating a Christ-centered blog or podcast where you deal solely with witnessing to others through writing and the Word, the potential to affect the world for Christ, just by living your Christian life out on a social networking site is endless as well.

In public, I use Instagram *as a way to reach unbelievers. See, I'm passionate about art and travel and try to find non-believing followers that way. I post my museum findings and tiny travel adventures, betting those with identical passions will want to see what I've seen. That's how I got the grandma from Italy to follow me. And the guy who makes unusual wood carvings. And the amateur photographer in Chicago. Then, about every three weeks, I post a Scripture, or a reminder to be kind and forgive, or something to make them laugh because it made me laugh. Then it's back to the art and travel posts. I do that because I figure they're more likely to listen to a fellow art lover/traveler than they are someone using the Internet solely to preach at them. My way is to let them know there are people just like them who love art, travel—and Jesus. And maybe that will be enough when they can choose to be civil or uncivil, or a spiritual crisis reminds them that someone out there believes in the power of prayer. Among the plentitude of accounts, it's a start. It's a seed. (Kent Curry in the blog "What God Hopes," posted by Debbie Simler-Goff.)

We live in a creative, expressive, amazing world. Information almost impossible to attain a few hundred years ago is now readily available with the click of a mouse or the tap of a few keys. Social networking sites make followers and friends privy to information such as what you had for breakfast, the song that's been stuck in your head, or the latest article you've been reading. It is easier to share your life, and, consequently, the good news than ever before.

What could you do through your social networking site of choice? Could you write a poem that hits the heart of a stranger who is a friend of one of your friends? Could you share an article that inspires others to look deeper into God's Word, or answers some probing questions they have had about faith? Could you sit in a stairwell and record a song that would cause a visitation of anointing on someone thousands of miles away, many days later? You could. But will you?

In the Workshop

Split your classroom up into groups of two to four. Assign each of them a different social media outlet to research from the following list:

| Facebook | Snapchat | Instagram | Twitter |
| YouTube | Blogs | Podcasts | |

After they have thoroughly researched their assigned form of media, have them formulate a plan for using it as an evangelism tool and share that plan with the rest of the class through a short two-minute presentation.

Final Inspection

1. What is the internet?

   _____
   _____
   _____
   _____

2. Why does the internet have potential for personal evangelism?

   _____
   _____
   _____
   _____

3. Have you used the internet for personal evangelism or to research a biblical topic? If yes, why? If no, why not?

4. What is your favorite internet tool (Facebook, Snapchat, Instagram, Twitter, YouTube, Blogs, Podcasts)? Why?

5. How do you envision yourself using the internet for evangelism?

Personal Study Notes

Lesson 4

Product Placement

Project Blueprints

After this lesson, students should be able to

- Understand the concept of "product placement"
- Know why observant Jews use mezuzahs and phylacteries
- Think of subtle ways to witness for Christ
- Comprehend the concepts of moderation and temperance in witnessing

In the Toolbox

Product placement: A practice in which manufacturers of goods or providers of a service gain exposure for their products by paying for them to be featured in movies and television programs.

In His Word

And thou shalt love the LORD thy God with all thine heart, and with all thy soul, and with all thy might. And these words, which I command thee this day, shall be in thine heart: and thou shalt teach them diligently unto thy children, and shalt talk of them when thou sittest in thine house, and when thou walkest by the way, and when thou liest down, and when thou risest up. And thou shalt bind them for a sign upon thine hand, and they shall be as frontlets between thine eyes. And thou shalt write them upon the posts of thy house, and on thy gates. (Deuteronomy 6:5–9)

Therefore shall ye lay up these my words in your heart and in your soul, and bind them for a sign upon your hand, that they may be as frontlets between your eyes. (Deuteronomy 11:18.)

My son, observe the commandment of your father and do not forsake the teaching of your mother; bind them continually on your heart; tie them around your neck. (Proverbs 6:20–21, NASB)

In Their Shoes

Monica tapped her foot impatiently, waiting for the woman in line in front of her at the checkout counter to finish placing her items on the conveyer belt. She had arrived at the checkout point the exact same time as the woman in question, offering graciously to allow her a chance to purchase her groceries first. Monica was holding three items in her hands, while the woman in front of her had forty-five to fifty separate items. Monica had assumed the woman would return her own kindness with the reasonable gesture of letting her check out first. That was not the case this day. Now Monica stood, watching the woman remove item after item from her cart. It was almost magical. It defied reason so many things would fit in that one small space. She knew she shouldn't, but every fiber of Monica's being cried out to make a sarcastic comment. She wouldn't do that, but perhaps one tiny eye roll.

As Monica wrestled with her inner demons, the conveyer belt finally moved forward enough for her to put her three items down to be scanned. She sighed softly to herself and smiled at the woman in front of her when she fumbled with her wallet, picking it up for her when it fell to the floor. Finally, the women bid both Monica and the cashier a good day as she exited the building.

"I'm so sorry about the delay," the cashier said to Monica. "Many people would not have been so patient."

"I require much patience from others," Monica responded. "It's imperative that I not only take patience but give it."

"Truth. By the way, I love your hat. Where did you get it?" Monica gestured to her red baseball cap that sported the stitched outline of the continent of Africa across its front.

"Oh this? I'm glad you like it; I love it as well. One of my friends is going on a summer missions trip to Tanzania and she's selling these to raise money for it."

"I think it's so awesome when people get to go to places like that."

"I do too. My friend has such a heart for helping people, but not just with their physical needs—their emotional and spiritual needs as well."

The cashier laughed to herself. "I wish someone would take it upon themselves to help me like that. It would be nice if there was someplace I could go here in the States to have my emotional and spiritual needs met."

"You know," Monica said as she pulled her church business card out of her wallet, "now that you mention it. . . ."

In Our Hands

According to historical tradition, the verses used at the beginning of this lesson from Deuteronomy and Proverbs were taken quite seriously by Jews of the biblical time period. (They are still taken seriously by practicing Jews today.) Jews literally take the Word of God and affix it to the doorposts of their houses as well as wearing it on their foreheads, right between their eyes during morning prayer services.

A *mezuzah* is a parchment inscribed with religious texts and attached in a case to the doorpost of a Jewish house as a sign of faith. Those practicing mainstream Rabbinic Judaism affix this to the doorposts of the home to fulfill the mitzvah (Biblical commandment) mentioned in Deuteronomy 6:9 (NASB): "Write them on the doorframes of your houses and on your gates."

They don't just post God's Word where it can be seen in their homes, however. They also wear it on their person. A *phylactery* is "a small leather box containing Hebrew texts on vellum, worn by Jewish men at morning prayer as a reminder to keep the law." A collective term for Jewish phylacteries is *tefillin*.

Myjewishlearning.com explains the use of tefillin this way:

The tefillin consist of two black leather boxes and straps to hold them on. One is worn on the biceps, and its strap, which is tied with a special knot, is wound by the wearer seven times around the forearm and hand—on the left arm for right-handed people and on the right for those who are left-handed. The second box is worn on the forehead at the hairline, with its straps going around the back of the head, connected at the top of the neck with a special knot, and hanging in front on each side.

Four passages in the Torah call upon the Israelites to keep God's words in mind by "binding them as a sign upon their hands and making them *totafot* (an enigmatic term) between (their) eyes." Tefillin, as ordained by the rabbinic leaders of classical Judaism, are intended to fulfill that commandment.

The tefillin are worn during morning services except on Shabbat or festivals. In Orthodox and Conservative congregations, most men wear tefillin, as do some women in Conservative congregations. The use of tefillin is less prominent in Reform and Reconstructionist congregations by both men and women. Inside the tefillin are handwritten parchments with texts from the four passages mentioned above.

Jews wear the Word of God on their foreheads to remind themselves not to forget it. Not only is such a thing a good reminder to them, but I would imagine an instantaneous open door of explanation and witness to the curious. Any time someone wants to know what they are wearing on their heads or why, what that tiny box in their doorway is or why, they have an opportunity to explain their faith, their God, and the prominence of His Word in their lives. What a beautiful practice and innovative witnessing tool!

There is seemingly no end to the influx of available Christian "product" or "gear." There are journals with Scripture on them, fish pendants to hang around our necks, "honk if you love Jesus" bumper stickers, wrist bands stamped with "WWJD," flags to hang up in our driveways, notecards to leave in books we borrow from the library, baseballs caps with the Last Supper etched onto them, T-shirts proclaiming the latest program we are promoting at our church, and billboards stretched across highways. You can purchase Christian blankets, books, pens, keychains, stationery, and jewelry almost anywhere blankets, books, pens, keychains, stationery, and jewelry are sold.

Should we take advantage of this to the fullest degree? Should all our new dresses bear the print of the cross upon them? Should we paint the outside of our houses with the good news that "Jesus saves"? Should we cover our vehicles in so many bumper stickers expounding upon the love of God that it's impossible to read them all when someone passes us in traffic?

We might look to the Word for the answer to those questions:

And beside this, giving all diligence, add to your faith virtue; and to virtue knowledge; and to knowledge temperance; and to temperance patience; and to patience godliness. (II Peter 1:5-6)

The definition of *temperance* is "moderation in thought, action, or feeling."

Rejoice in the Lord alway: and again I say, Rejoice. Let your moderation be known unto all men. The Lord is at hand. Be careful for nothing; but in everything by prayer and supplication with thanksgiving let your requests be made known to God. And the peace of God, which passeth all understanding, shall keep your hearts and minds through Christ Jesus. (Philippians 4:4-7)

The definition of *moderation* is "the avoidance of excess or extremes, especially in one's behavior or political opinions."

Before you spray paint John 3:16 across your front porch, put the spray paint can down and consider the idea of moderation in all things. So if we're not to adapt a "Go big or go home" mentality in our "product placement," and we are attempting to use this tool with moderation and wisdom, how are we to operate wisely?

For this answer, we look to a place we rarely look to for inspiration or instruction. We look to Hollywood. If anyone knows about product placement, it's the entertainment industry. Since movies began being made, companies have been paying production companies to feature products in their films and shows in subtle ways.

In the beginning of 2018, Toyota featured their newest automobile in the film *The Black Panther*. In a scene involving seven hundred people and one hundred and fifty cars, the blue Lexus LC 500 stood out as the car the hero was using to chase the bad guys. When the trailer for the movie dropped in the fall of 2017, the few seconds the car was featured in it received eighty-nine million views within twenty-four hours. How many people were exposed to this product by viewing the movie? It's hard to track an exact number, but as of the time of this writing, the film had made 1.1 billion dollars in the box office. It's safe to say a few people had seen it. Because Toyota does not waste time or money and has a clear way of tracking how advertisement affects sales, it is also safe to say this form of product placement has paid off ("The Marvellous Marketing Vehicle for the New Lexus" by Christian Sylt).

If Toyota feels it is worth their while to spend hundreds of thousands of dollars to advertise their car in a new movie, might it not be worth our while to "advertise" our faith some of the same ways?

We are not required to wear a banner with the phrase "I am a Christian!" blazing in bold letters across it, but the slightest opportunity to express our faith can be turned into an open door of epic proportions.

In closing, look up, listen to, and consider the words of the song "I Wanna Thank You" by Karen Peck and New River and begin to open your mind and heart to the possibility that the slightest seed sown might make an eternal difference in the life of someone you encounter in your world today.

In the Workshop

Provide your class with Christian "products" to test out during the week (T-shirts, stickers, keychains, baseball caps, and such like). Assign them the task of using at least one of these means of advertisement for five days. Have them keep track of people's reactions, conversations that were sparked by these products, as well as ideas for new ways to create and implement subtle (and spiritual) "product placement" in the world around them.

Final Inspection

1. Define "product placement."

2. How does one's attitude relate to product placement?

3. What are positive uses of Christian "products"?

4. Can "Christian products" have a downside? If so, how?

5. What is your "product placement" idea to evangelize your neighbor?

Lesson 5

Prayer-Centric Evangelism

Project Blueprints

After this lesson, students should be able to

- Tell the story of Philip and the eunuch
- Realize the need to be sensitive to the leading of the Spirit
- Experience being led by the Spirit
- Understand how prayer can work in evangelism.

In the Toolbox

Prayer: An address (such as a petition) to God or a god in word or thought, a set order of words used in praying, an earnest request or wish

In His Word

And when they bring you unto the synagogues, and unto magistrates, and powers, take ye no thought how or what thing ye shall answer, or what ye shall say: for the Holy Ghost shall teach you in the same hour what ye ought to say. (Luke 12:11–12)

Rejoice evermore. Pray without ceasing. In everything give thanks: for this is the will of God in Christ Jesus concerning you. (I Thessalonians 5:16–18)

Be careful for nothing; but in every thing by prayer and supplication with thanksgiving let your requests be made known unto God. (Philippians 4:6)

I exhort therefore, that, first of all, supplications, prayers, intercessions, and giving of thanks, be made for all men; for kings, and for all that are in authority; that we may lead a quiet and peaceable life in all godliness and honesty. For this is good and acceptable in the sight of God our Saviour; who will have all men to be saved, and to come unto the knowledge of the truth. (I Timothy 2:1-4)

In Their Shoes

Vicky stood in line at the grocery store, behind a woman who had more than enough paper towels to stock an entire school cafeteria. Before Vicky had gotten out of bed that morning, she had prayed, asking the Lord to lead her to people in need of Him. Something pricked her mind, urging her to pay closer attention to the woman in front of her. The woman turned, apologizing for the amount of items crowding the conveyor belt.

As she did, Vicky heard a clear voice in her head: "Ask her if something is going on in her life." Vicky immediately attempted to suppress the urge to act on the voice. What kind of person asks a woman standing in line with them in the grocery store if "something is going on in her life"? She made an effort to do anything else: re-arrange her purse; flip through her wallet; check her cellphone for new messages. The voice would not relent. She knew with a certainty she needed to ask the woman if something was going on in her life. So she took a deep breath, gathered all of her courage, made eye contact with the woman, and said the words: "Hi. I know this might sound strange, but I wanted to ask you. Is there something going on in your life?"

The woman immediately burst into tears. Right there in the checkout line, she told Vicky all about her son, who was in critical condition at a local hospital and how she had just been wishing with all her might there was someone to share her situation with. That someone would just approach her and take an interest in her life and her situation. None of her friends seemed to notice her distress; none of her family understood it. She had been wishing someone would ask her what was going on so she could share the terrible burden.

The lady said she knew this conversation had not occurred by chance, and she asked Vicky to visit her son in the hospital. After paying for her groceries, Vicky got the name of the hospital and the room number where the son was staying and pledged to do just that—visit him.

Later that day, Vicky arrived at room 102 in Haven of Hope Hospital on the north side of town. She, along with her friend Joe, knocked on a stranger's door. After explaining who they were and why they had come to visit the sick young man, they sat back in amazement listening to this young man's story.

He was actually a backslidden Pentecostal. He had come into the church and out of it just as easily in his younger years. Now that the debilitating illness had gripped his body, he had been lying in the hospital for months feeling like no one loved him, no one cared, and he had gone too far to ever return. Yet the Lord had sent some people of that same faith to find him in the hospital and remind him that he was never too far from grace—not to mention sending Vicky into the life of a mother who would never forget the supernatural events of the day, or the Lord's personal care over her life and the life of her son.

In Our Hands

The story above, as with most of the stories in this textbook, is based on true events. More stories like it are almost everywhere you look. They are real-life scenarios where the Lord used prayer to lead people to the actions and interactions that would best portray His glory in the world. They are stories where people followed the leading of the Spirit straight into a testimony.

During my first year back in the United States, for example, I felt a burden for the janitorial staff working at the world headquarters of the UPCI. I couldn't bear the thought of them working in that building day after day but perhaps never encountering the truth for themselves or knowing its power. I prayed about what to do, and I felt I should bake cupcakes for them and invite them to our church's Christmas program. I did this, taking extra care to make a variety of cupcakes from scratch and decorate them as beautifully as I could. If the Lord told me to make cupcakes, I would do so with all my might.

When the day came to deliver them, I arrived at the janitorial closet to find no one there. I couldn't find one single member of the cleaning crew in the entire building that day. Discouraged, I left a note on the cupcakes, thanking the janitors for their service and reminding them they were valued by me and loved by the Lord.

I didn't think much about it after that. I wrote the note, left the cupcakes, and walked away, never knowing if anyone even discovered them before the Christmas season was over. Almost a year later, a member of the cleaning staff was prayed through by Ryan O'Neil in the world headquarters chapel. Much rejoicing filled Heaven as this precious soul found love and the Lord, and I was so delighted to hear of it. The week after this happened, my mother ran into the woman who had experienced salvation. She congratulated her, and when she did, the woman said, "Thank you. And, by the way, would you please thank your daughter for those cupcakes?"

I did not have the ability to work hand in hand with the members of the janitorial staff. I couldn't stand by their side and expound upon Scripture to them daily, any more than I could construct a pop-up tent in the business lobby and preach loud sermons. But I could follow the leading of the Spirit. I could make cupcakes.

> I have planted, Apollos watered; but God gave the increase. So then neither is he that planteth any thing, neither he that watereth; but God that giveth the increase. Now he that planteth and he that watereth are one: and every man shall receive his own reward according to his own labour. (I Corinthians 3:6–8)

You never know the difference the simple part you played might make in the Kingdom. It is so important to walk through each day with prayer, because any chance encounter might make a difference in the eternal life of another human being. The Lord is working all the time.

Consider the story about a woman who was standing in line at a restaurant. She felt instinctively that she should pay the bill for the friend in the restaurant with her. She struggled with the thought, because the money she had was her grocery money for the month. However, she felt the urging of the Holy Spirit so strongly that she did what God had asked, making a difference in her friend's life and opening a door to bless and to witness to her. She wasn't just caring for the needy; she was listening to the voice of the Spirit of God, remaining faithful in even the small things.

When you open your hands to bless others, the door to blessing in your own life often swings wide as well. The very next day that woman was shopping at Kohl's, and she purchased a toy mask on sale. Playing with this childish toy filled her with so much joy that she posted a video of herself laughing on the internet. By the time she woke up the next morning, that video had gone viral. Candace Payne, an unknown worship leader before this incident, became a face people now recognize in the streets, instantaneously gaining a platform on every major news network and talk show, even signing a book deal. Now she has a vast stage to witness to others for the glory of God, all because she was faithful in the small things.

Speaking of Candace:

And the angel of the Lord spake unto Philip, saying, Arise, and go toward the south unto the way that goeth down from Jerusalem unto Gaza, which is desert. And he arose and went: and, behold, a man of Ethiopia, an eunuch of great authority under Candace queen of the Ethiopians, who had the charge of all her treasure, and had come to Jerusalem for to worship, was retuning, and sitting in his chariot read Esaias the prophet. Then the Spirit said unto Philip, Go near, and join thyself to this chariot. And Philip ran thither to him, and heard him read the prophet Esaias, and said, Understandest thou what thou readest? And he said, How can I, except some man should guide me? And he desired Philip that he would come up and sit with him. The place of the scripture which he read was this, He was led as a sheep to the slaughter; and like a lamb dumb before his shearer, so opened he not his mouth: in his humiliation his judgment was taken away: and who shall declare his generation? for his life is taken from the earth. And the eunuch answered Philip, and said, I pray thee, of whom speaketh the prophet this? of himself, or of some other man? Then Philip opened his mouth, and began at the same scripture, and preached unto him Jesus. And as they went on their way, they came unto a certain water: and the eunuch said,

> See, here is water; what doth hinder me to be baptized? And Philip said, if thou believest with all thine heart, thou mayest. And he answered and said, I believe that Jesus Christ is the Son of God. And he commanded the chariot to stand still: and they went down both into the water, both Philip and the eunuch; and he baptized him. (Acts 8:26–38)

Because Philip was sensitive to the Spirit of God in prayer, the Lord led him directly to someone who was in desperate need of the gospel and ready to receive it. That wasn't all.

> And when they were come up out of the water, the Spirit of the Lord caught away Philip, that the eunuch saw him no more: and he went on his way rejoicing. But Philip was found at Azotus: and passing through he preached in all the cities, till he came to Caesarea. (Acts 8:39–40)

Because Philip was willing to be led of the Spirit, the Lord was able to move him at lightning speed to exactly where he needed to go. God longs to have that same experience with us. He wants us to be willing to go where He sends us without question or hesitation and to do what He commands without fear. He wants us, through sensitivity to the Spirit, to be led right to those who need Him, straight out into the fields ripe for harvest.

In the Workshop

Challenge your class to pray every single morning this next week, and for that prayer to be geared specifically toward evangelism. Encourage them to follow the leading of the Lord even in the most subtle and miniscule ways and to chart the things He does in and through them even in the short span of a week. Invite them to ask the Lord to blow their minds this week, believe with them that He will, and rejoice together as a unit when the reports role in.

Final Inspection

1. Describe your prayer life.

2. Has the Lord led you into situations such as Vicky experienced? If yes, what happened?

3. What would have happened if Philip had not been sensitive to the Spirit?

4. Based on I Timothy 2:1–4, make a list of people you need to pray for.

5. How has God led you to go out of your way to witness to someone?

Personal Study Notes

Lesson 6

A Lifestyle of Holiness

Project Blueprints

After this lesson, students should be able to

- Define biblical holiness
- Discuss the value of standards of holiness
- Understand how standards of holiness can capture someone's attention
- Respond appropriately when asked about standards of holiness

In the Toolbox

Holiness: The state of being holy

Standard: Used or accepted as normal or average, also a flag or emblem a troop carries into battle

In His Word

For I am the LORD who brought you up out of the land of Egypt to be your God. You shall therefore be holy, for I am holy. (Leviticus 11:45, ESV)

Strive for peace with everyone, and for the holiness without which no one will see the Lord. (Hebrews 12:14, ESV)

But as he who called you is holy, you also be holy in all your conduct, since it is written, "You shall be holy, for I am holy. (I Peter 1:15–16, ESV)

He has saved us and called us to a holy life—not because of anything we have done but because of his own purpose and grace. This grace was given us in Christ Jesus before the beginning of time. (II Timothy 1:9, NIV)

Therefore, I urge you, brothers and sisters, in view of God's mercy, to offer your bodies as a living sacrifice, holy and pleasing to God— this is your true and proper worship. (Romans 12:1, NIV)

In Their Shoes

Laura sat in the small group of believers that met at her church every Friday night. The group had been doing a short series on discipleship. She enjoyed the rigorous and passionate discussion of her peers on that topic as they came up with new ideas to reach people or mulled over what being a true disciple maker meant. Tonight they were discussing places one might encounter someone to disciple.

Tom raised his hand and mentioned his little sister had started running in the park in order to make new friends and meet those who needed Christ. Laura sighed quietly to herself. She had grown up in the church, attended a private, church-run school, and now her full-time job consisted of working as a church receptionist. Almost everyone Laura interacted with daily was already churched.

Several months prior, she had been praying about ways to meet people and she too had come up with the idea of running in the park. Laura was by no means athletic and running (or even walking) any great distance did not appeal to her in the slightest. She had a burden for those who didn't know the Lord, however, and was determined to do what she could to reach them.

In order to reach them, she would have to actually meet them. It seemed an obvious step one. So Laura spoke to her friend Carol, and Carol agreed to join forces with her and keep her accountable to running every Saturday. Laura and Carol had been faithfully running in the park for six months, and they had not forged a friendship with anyone. People didn't show up to run consistently, and when they did, they were always running so fast. It would be awkward to chase after them, clutching church tracts in their fists as the paper waved wildly in the wind.

Laura was grateful for this discussion, and she knew the need was great. She also was convinced that going to where the people were in order to meet and get to know them was a good idea. She nodded encouragingly and smiled at Tom across the room. Hopefully his little sister would have better luck making a contact through exercise than she and Carol had had so far.

The very next day, with the thoughts of a six-month streak of failure heavy on her mind, Laura put on her running clothes. It was sure to be blazing hot outside, but Laura and Carol consistently dressed as modestly on the track as they did off it. While everyone else whizzed past them in comfortable shorts and tank tops, they sweated into their long sleeves and skirts. But they were proud to do it. They didn't mind wearing their love for their God in their uncut hair or on their T-shirts.

Laura laced up her running shoes and prayed, as she did at the beginning of every single trip to the track, that the Lord would send her and Carol someone to befriend and to witness to, and then she headed off to meet Carol. The girls met at the track and were warming up to get started when, for the first time in six months, they were approached by a stranger. He said, "Hi. I've been meaning to ask you, every time you are out here, it's so HOT! What are you wearing and why?"

In Our Hands

In the above true story, Laura—who happens to be me—was attempting to do her part to be a witness. She showed up. She tried to reach out to people. When it looked like everything she was doing was destined for failure, she was a witness through her standards of holiness. The Lord opened a door through her obedience to His Word, and it turned out she was a walking billboard for His name and fame wherever she went, just because of her standards of holiness.

The Lord requires us to be holy as He is holy. Consequently, we practice many different holiness standards.

We do not wear jewelry.

Your beauty should not come from outward adornment, such as elaborate hairstyles and the wearing of gold jewelry or fine clothes. Rather, it should be that of your inner self, the unfading beauty of a gentle and quiet spirit, which is of great worth in God's sight. For this is the way the holy women of the past who put their hope in God used to adorn themselves. They submitted themselves to their own husbands. (I Peter 3:2–5, NIV)

We wear clothing pertaining to our gender, without putting on apparel that is a man's if we are a woman, or a woman's if we are a man.

A woman must not wear men's clothing, nor a man wear women's clothing, for the LORD your God detests anyone who does this. (Deuteronomy 22:5, NIV)

Women do not cut their hair, whereas men do.

Be ye followers of me, even as I also am of Christ. Now I praise you, brethren, that ye remember me in all things, and keep the ordinances, as I delivered them to you. But I would have you know, that the head of every man is Christ; and the head of the woman is the man; and the head of Christ is God. Every man praying or prophesying, having his head covered, dishonoureth his head. But every woman that prayeth or prophesieth with her head uncovered dishonoureth her head: for that is even all one as if she were shaven. For if the woman be not covered, let her also be shorn: but if it be a shame for a woman to be shorn or shaven, let her be covered. For a man indeed ought not to cover his head, forasmuch as he is the image and glory of God: but the woman is the glory of the man. For the man is not of the woman: but the woman of the man. Neither was the man created for the woman; but the woman for the man. For

> this cause ought the woman to have power on her head because of the angels. (I Corinthians 11:1–10)

These are just a few of the signs of outward holiness. They do not in any way negate the work of inward holiness, but they are outward signs that we as believers are completely surrendered and submitted to Someone else. They are practices we engage in because we love Him. A woman should be proud to manifest that love in her uncut hair and declare it with her dress. A man should be proud to proclaim his love for the Lord in dress and behavior pertaining to and becoming for a man. These are our "standards."

A "standard" is the way we do things that could be "used or accepted as normal." Standard. Just how it is. However, a standard can also mean a flag or emblem that a troop would carry into battle. During times of war, the standard would be used to locate a soldier's group, so he would know how to find it if he got separated. It would also be a signal to the enemy of exactly what they stood for and were fighting for.

Polybius remarked in his work *The Histories* that the signifier, the person who carried the standard in battle, was "the bravest and most vigorous among the soldiers." "Ask History" on the website *Reddit* tells us the purpose of a standard-bearer (or signifier) was to give the unit's members a visual signal as to where the unit was. If you were separated from your unit in battle, you would search for the standard.

The standard-bearer was normally the closest to the unit leader. If the standard "fell," the rest of the unit would not know where to return to and it was likely the leader had fallen as well. "Loss of a standard in battle was considered to be one of the worst things to happen—the Honor of the unit was lost." (https://www.reddit.com/r/AskHistorians/comments/21f4us/how_the . . .) Capturing the standard of an opposing unit in battle was considered to be a great victory.

We know life is more than what meets the eye. A constant war is raging around us for our souls and the souls of those we might eventually witness to.

> For we wrestle not against flesh and blood, but against principalities, against powers, against the rulers of the darkness of this world, against spiritual wickedness in high places. (Ephesians 6:12)

As we journey through life, more is going on than meets the eye. However, my firm belief is that what meets the eye can also make a difference in life. The natural informs of the supernatural. Just like a troop in ancient battle, we hold up a standard in warfare. We proudly walk in standards of holiness, letting everyone we meet know something is different about us. The standards signify what we stand for. The standards also signify our physical position. The closer we are to the standard, the closer we are to the leader.

> So shall they fear the name of the LORD from the west, and his glory from the rising of the sun. When the enemy shall come in like a flood, the Spirit of the LORD shall lift up a standard against him. (Isaiah 59:19)

When the standard rises, no one doubts who the army belongs to or what it stands for. It is a bold proclamation. You can be a walking witness for God without saying a word, drawing people to Him the minute you enter an atmosphere if you are carrying the standard with you, making you automatically close to the one who leads us into His kingdom. Holiness standards are a proclamation of belief at immediate sight, and the doors they open into evangelism are endless.

In the Workshop

Distribute pieces of paper and markers or crayons to your students. Show them pictures of medieval battle standards you have pulled from the internet. Encourage them to design a "battle standard" of their own and then write some standards of holiness they are committed to following on the back.

Final Inspection

1. During war, what is the purpose of the unit's standard?

2. What is the purpose of standards of holiness?

3. What is your personal definition of biblical holiness?

4. How can holiness standards be used in evangelism?

5. How would you respond if a stranger asked about your appearance?

Personal Study Notes

Lesson 7

Radio Evangelism

Project Blueprints

After this lesson, students should be able to

- Appreciate the miracle of radio
- Understand the potential of radio evangelism
- Discuss ways Christian radio can be used on a local basis
- Track the impact of Christian radio locally

In the Toolbox

Radio: The transmission and reception of electromagnetic waves of radio frequency, especially those carrying sound messages.

Radio waves: An electromagnetic wave of a frequency between about 10^4 and 10^{11} or 10^{12} Hz, as used for long-distance communication.

In His Word

Sing to the Lord, bless His name; proclaim the good news of His salvation from day to day. Declare His glory among the nations, His wonders among all peoples. For the Lord is great and greatly to be praised; He is to be feared above all gods. (Psalm 96:2–4, NKJV)

As you go, proclaim this message: "The kingdom of heaven has come near." (Matthew 10:7, NIV)

For I am not ashamed of the gospel, because it is the power of God that brings salvation to everyone who believes: first to the Jew, then to the Gentile. (Romans 1:16, NIV)

In Their Shoes

Ryan sat in the restaurant feeling all alone. This last fight with his parents was the worst of all. He wasn't sure they would ever recover. If they didn't recover, he would lose their financial support. If he lost their financial support, he didn't know where he would live, what he would do, or how he would feed his crippling drug habit. No one cared about him. He knew that with certainty.

His parents were sick and tired of dealing with his antics and failures. His friends stuck around only to use him and his parents' money. He knew that with certainty too; though he was good at ignoring it. His sister had no desire to be around him. She was a successful Harvard graduate, a businesswoman. She only took time for people who made something of themselves, who brought something of value to the table. She wasted no opportunity to remind Ryan he brought nothing to the table at all. As if he needed to be reminded.

Ryan briefly considered ordering everything on the menu and just eating until he died. Or going back to his car and taking all the drugs hidden there at once, bringing on death that way. Hey, he might not even make it back to the car. He might just throw himself into traffic on the way there. No one cared. No one wanted him. And no matter what he did, he could not seem to succeed in life. He was a failure in every sense of the word. He failed at school. He failed at home. He failed in friendship. He definitely failed at romance. He failed at family. Even the people who were supposed to love him no matter what were tired of seeing his face.

Ryan signaled to the waiter he was ready for the bill. The smiling restaurant employee approached him without a check in hand.

"Your bill has been taken care of."

"What?"

"Your bill has been taken care of. You've been joyed."

"Excuse me?"

"You've been joyed."

"I'm sorry, I've been WHAT?"

"Oh. I guess you haven't heard the expression. We get this in here all the time. There's this radio station, 99.1 JOY FM, and they have this practice where they encourage people to pay for the person behind them in line, or sneak grab people's bills in restaurants, just to show them the love of God. Just to remind them they aren't alone and someone cares about them. To share joy with strangers."

"Why would they want to share joy with strangers?"

"I don't know . . . I guess it's less about what they want and more about showing people God loves them, and they aren't alone. If you really believe in God, I think it's natural to follow His heart like that."

"Hmm. . . . What was the name of that radio station?"

"99.1 JOY FM."

Ryan left the restaurant, saying the station number repeatedly in his head. Could it be coincidence that when he was feeling so lost and hopeless, someone stepped in to let him know they cared? He would have to see what this was all about. Upon arriving at his car, he immediately turned the radio dial to the appropriate station. As the sound waves flooded his vehicle, he immediately began to cry as love, almost as if with tangible arms, enveloped him. The song said, "Oh the overwhelming, never ending, reckless love of God. Oh it chases me down, fights till I'm found, leaves the ninety-nine . . ." ("Reckless Love" by Cory Asbury).

In Our Hands

Two things changed my view on the impact radio evangelism could have on the world. The first was that I began listening to 99.1 JOY FM on a regular basis. It's a listener-supported Christian radio station in my town, and it's incredibly popular. A lot of evidence supports America's turn from God, but I've seen enough JOY FM stickers today alone to argue people are also turning toward Him. In between songs, the announcers share testimonies of people being changed by what they heard on air, or people call in with their personal testimonies. The impact one radio station has made for the kingdom of God is great indeed. I had not realized radio evangelism could be so far reaching.

The second thing was my reading *When God Doesn't Fix It* by Laura Story. In her book she shares the journey she and her husband walked through with an illness he has.

She *also* shares the unexpected impact a song she wrote called "Blessings" has had on radio audiences. She relays testimony after testimony from radio listeners. One couple had been pregnant with twin boys when one of the children died in the womb. The other was inconsolable without his brother and spent the majority of his little life crying. It turned out he suffered from a brain injury that would ultimately leave him without sight or speech. When the couple heard Laura's song on the radio, they were given the strength and comfort they needed, their trust in God was renewed, and their marriage was strengthened.

Her song consoled a woman living without her only desire since birth—a child—in a five-year-long struggle with infertility. A woman played "Blessings" at the memorial service of her miscarried, unborn baby, and wrote Laura to inform her the song kept her going again when she lost a second child.

Laura's song has helped people whose husbands have left, whose friends have abandoned them, and whose lives are falling apart. The song has impacted men battling terminal illness. A little girl with half a heart, spending the majority of her time in the hospital, was given wisdom beyond her years by listening to the song.

A young man who was wrestling with drugs and alcohol had a mother who would pray over his car every day. On one occasion, his iPod cord was not working and the only station he could get on the radio was the local Christian station. Laura's song began to play, and when it did, he began to cry. He said, "The words hit me and I realized who I was becoming. I went into rehab that day and changed my life. I knew God was with me. Thank you for the song. I'm not sure where I would be without it."

The stories go on and on of the backsliders returning, hearts being strengthened, and people turning to God all because Laura's song was on the radio.

Something is significant about the good news of the gospel being proclaimed on the air. Here's how radio waves work, according to the dictionary:

> The radio waves travel through the air at the speed of light. When the waves arrive at the receiver antenna, they make electrons vibrate inside it. This produces an electric current that recreates the original signal. Transmitter and receiver antennas are often very similar in design.

Satan is often referred to as the "prince of the air."

> Wherein in time past ye walked according to the course of this world, according to the prince of the power of the air, the spirit that now worketh in the children of disobedience. (Ephesians 2:2)

We know that he has a throne:

> I know where you dwell, where Satan's throne is. Yet you hold fast my name, and you did not deny my faith even in the days of Antipas my faithful witness, who was killed among you, where Satan dwells. (Revelation 2:13, ESV)

We know he has a kingdom:

> And if Satan casts out Satan, he is divided against himself. How then will his kingdom stand?" (Matthew 12:26, ESV)

The most he might ever be is a prince. He certainly cannot be King. There is only one of those.

"Which he will display at the proper time—he who is the blessed and only Sovereign, the King of kings and the Lord of lords. (I Timothy 6:15, ESV)

Satan was known even in the time of Jesus to be a prince.

But the Pharisees said, "He casts out demons by the prince of demons." (Matthew 9:34, ESV)

So Satan, the prince of the air and of the demons, does have some measure of authority given to him by God. A prime example of this would be when Jesus was tempted in the desert and Satan said to him:

And said to him, "To you I will give all this authority and their glory, for it has been delivered to me, and I give it to whom I will." (Luke 4:6, ESV)

But there are many other examples.

So to keep me from becoming conceited because of the surpassing greatness of the revelations, a thorn was given me in the flesh, a messenger of Satan to harass me, to keep me from becoming conceited. (II Corinthians 12:7, ESV)

Then should not this woman, a daughter of Abraham, whom Satan bound for eighteen long years, be set free on the Sabbath day from what bound her? (Luke 13:16, NIV)

We know that we are from God, and the whole world lies in the power of the evil one. (I John 5:19, ESV)

We are from God, but the whole world lies in the power of the evil one. This is the prince of the air. What happens, I wonder, when the very air itself is used to proclaim the message of the goodness of God? Can the atmosphere itself be changed by praise and worship? Consider these biblical examples:

And it came to pass, when the priests were come out of the holy place, that the cloud filled the house of the LORD. (I Kings 8:10)

So the priests sent worship up to God, and when that was through, a tangible cloud filled the house, literally changing the atmosphere.

Another example of this would be when young David played the harp for Saul.

> And it came to pass, when the evil spirit from God was upon Saul, that David took an harp, and played with his hand: so Saul was refreshed, and was well, and the evil spirit departed from him. (I Samuel 16:23)

If David playing a harp in worship could vanquish evil spirits, and priests worshiping God in the Holy of Holies could bring down a tangible glory cloud, what must the Word of God sung, spoken, and sent out over the airways do to the atmosphere of the spirit world? Radio evangelism is an often-overlooked but incredibly powerful tool to combat the darkness of this world, lift the spirit of God's people, and bring to Him those who are lost and searching.

In the Workshop

Encourage your class to spend at least ten minutes a day this week listening to Christian radio. What is being said on the air on those stations? What is the overarching theme of the songs? Are there testimonies from listeners? What is the station doing well? In what ways could the impact of the station be used? How can your students use Christian radio as a tool for witnessing to their friends? Encourage them to keep a log of their thoughts as they listen, returning the next week with their observations and findings.

Final Inspection

1. Do you listen to Christian radio? If yes, why? If no, why not?

   _____
   _____
   _____
   _____

2. If you listen to Christian radio, has a song or a sermon ministered to you in a special way? If so, how?

3. Do you see any potential in you personally becoming involved in Christian radio? How?

4. What are the drawbacks or downsides of using radio evangelism?

5. If Satan is the prince of the air, how can we hinder his influence?

Lesson 8

Hospitality

Project Blueprints

After this lesson, students should be able to

- Describe hospitality
- Cite biblical examples of hospitality
- Understand how hospitality can lead to evangelism
- Purpose to be hospitable

In the Toolbox

Hospitality: The friendly and generous reception and entertainment of guests, visitors, or strangers.

In His Word

Rejoice in hope, be patient in tribulation, be constant in prayer. Contribute to the needs of the saints and seek to show hospitality. (Romans 12:12–13, ESV)

And is well known for her good deeds, such as bringing up children, showing hospitality, washing the feet of the Lord's people, helping those in trouble and devoting herself to all kinds of good deeds. (I Timothy 5:10, NIV)

Rather, he must be hospitable, one who loves what is good, who is self-controlled, upright, holy and disciplined. (Titus 1:8, NIV)

Above all, love each other deeply, because love covers over a multitude of sins. Offer hospitality to one another without grumbling. (I Peter 4:8–9, NIV)

Share with the Lord's people who are in need. Practice hospitality. (Romans 12:13, NIV)

Show hospitality to one another without grumbling. (I Peter 4:9, ESV)

Let brotherly love continue. Do not neglect to show hospitality to strangers, for thereby some have entertained angels unawares. (Hebrews 13:1–2, ESV)

In Their Shoes

John wanted so desperately to share the good news of Jesus with those around him, but he just didn't have the financial means to do so. He and Laura had moved to a new town to establish a new life for themselves soon after they were married. Marriage was wonderful, and God's hand of blessing was on their lives, but money was tight.

John had long been pondering the biblical command to "love his neighbor" and praying for a way he could put that command into practice. The easiest thing, he knew, would be to open their home and invite their neighbors for a meal, but he and Laura could barely feed themselves, much less their neighborhood.

An amazing thing happened one Sunday though. The preacher used a parable about something called "stone soup." Someone who was hungry started making a pot of soup with nothing but a stone in it, and then people, one by one, added and added various ingredients into the soup until it was enough to feed a whole village.

John and Laura were ecstatic. They knew they didn't have the money to throw a lavish party or to serve their friends a five- or six-course meal, but they could make "stone soup." So John set to work informing his neighbors of his idea. One of his friends provided carrots, another some spices, another some stew meat, one family—tomatoes, another family—onions, until John and Laura had the ingredients of a beautiful stew for their neighborhood, and they opened their home.

There was much laughter that night over the "stone soup" the neighborhood enjoyed, crammed into John and Laura's small home. Someone finally asked John, "Why did you feel the need to open up your home to us when you have so little to give?"

John told them the truth. He told them he couldn't get away from the need to be hospitable to his neighbors. He told them God had loved and blessed him so much—opening His arms wide to him with love and acceptance—that he felt a burning desire to do the same thing.

That wasn't the only truth John was able to share that night. He was able to tell all his neighbors of the love of Jesus. That He died on the cross to set men free, and that if we have repented, are buried with Him in baptism, and are full of the Holy Ghost, we will spend eternity in Heaven with the Lord.

Two of John's friends didn't want to wait. They wanted the power of God inside of them as soon as possible. So the group of neighbors prayed, and as they did, the two men were filled with the Holy Ghost, right there in John's small living room. All because he and Laura had open hearts of hospitality. All because he and Laura opened their home.

In Our Hands

I don't know how you imagine Jesus, but I always see Him with His arms wide open. Throughout everything we read in Scripture, we see this Man was a welcoming man. Sick, poor, children, women, widowed, people from other classes and countries—He welcomed them all. He may not have spent much time in His house, but we can definitively declare Him as hospitable.

> Jesus radically challenges the disciples' expectations by over-stepping boundaries to invite people in. Hospitality has us seeing people as Jesus sees them and seeing Jesus in the people God brings before us.
> —Robert Schnase

We have many modern ideas of what hospitality should look like. Does it include a lavish party? Should we prepare to knock down walls in our house to make room for strangers? The New Testament Greek word for hospitality is *philoxenia*, which is a combination of the words "love" and "stranger." If you have love for strangers, that's hospitality. Extending open arms, welcoming people into your actual life and dwelling place—no matter what that looks like—is practicing hospitality effectively.

The blog "Ministry Matters" refers to a pastor, Olu Brown, and how, when he was traveling with his ball team, they would send one person into a restaurant to check out the surroundings after games. How was the hospitality? Could they accommodate all the team's players? If the scout determined the hospitality was good and the team could be accommodated, he would stick his head out of the door, calling the rest of the team inside. It only took one person to say, "We are welcome here. Our needs will be met here," for the restaurant to experience abundant business that day. The restaurant didn't have to go overboard with advertising, just operate with integrity, meet the needs of its customers, and welcome them inside.

If our homes, our churches, and our schools are hospitable—if they meet the needs of the people who come to them and welcome them inside—one satisfied and fully loved person can bring scores of other souls into our buildings. It is perhaps for this reason that Steve Childers calls hospitality the "key to evangelism in the 21st century." John Piper calls it "strategic hospitality," and he says we should be asking these questions: "How can I draw the most people into a deep experience of God's hospitality by the use of my home? Who are the people who could be brought together in my home most strategically for the sake of the kingdom?"

Everything we do should be hospitable, and all our ministries and churches should be places of hospitality. However, something is significant about the hospitality that happens in your own home.

> One day Elisha went to Shunem. And a well-to-do woman was there, who urged him to stay for a meal. So whenever he came by, he stopped there to eat. She said to her husband, "I know that this man who often comes our way is a holy man of God. Let's make a small room on the roof and put in it a bed and a table, a chair and a lamp for him. Then he can stay there whenever he comes to us." (II Kings 4:8–10, NIV)

We all know the rest of the story. (If you don't, it can be found in II Kings 4.) This woman opened up her household with hospitality and received unspeakable levels of blessing because of it. She received a son even in her husband's old age. When her son became gravely ill, she reached out to the prophet who had experienced the hospitality of her own home, and his prayers brought the boy to life. But besides being something that brings blessing—as we have just witnessed in II Kings 4—and a common practice in both Old and New Testaments ("Gaius, whose hospitality I and the whole church here enjoy, sends you his greetings" Romans 16:23, NIV), the Bible gives examples of hospitality directly leading to salvation.

> At that hour of the night the jailer took them and washed their wounds; then immediately he and all his household were baptized. The jailer brought them into his house and set a meal before them; he was filled with joy because he had come to believe in God—he and his whole household. (Acts 16:33–34, NIV)

Here we see a circumstance where a jailer took some prisoners home and washed their wounds. Because of this, a whole household came to know the Lord. Many cases we read in Scripture include people and "their whole households." That would not occur, if households were not open.

These examples, of course, include a believer opening his or her home, and then nonbelievers opening their homes with great results. Why should we, as believers, open our homes to nonbelievers? Jim Ozier feels the direct relationship between hospitality and evangelism can be found in Mark 1:17. "And Jesus said unto them, Come ye after me, and I will make you to become fishers of men."

Ozier outlines three principles to follow in hospitable evangelism:

1. If we follow Jesus, we'll be hospitable like He was. We are to model the openness and welcoming attitude of Jesus to all we meet.
2. Fish first in the pond you know best. Hospitality begins at home; open your life to the people you know and care about.
3. Fishers who love to fish love to fish in new waters. People who love to fish are constantly seeking a new lake. Just as people who love to evangelize are constantly seeking new places and ways to share the gospel.

Matt Chandler said: "Hospitable people tend to share the gospel well." This stands the test of reason. Those who are used to opening their hearts and homes will have an easier time sharing the gospel. Jesus was constantly inviting people in, opening His arms, and sharing whatever He had with those in need. When He welcomed people into His life, they welcomed Him into their hearts. The same will hold true today. Welcome people into your life, and they will welcome Jesus into their hearts.

In the Workshop

Encourage your class to practice hospitality this week. Suggest they invite someone to visit their home or take someone out to dinner. Allow them to split into groups to brainstorm ways they will put the tool of hospitality to good use, make plans, and set goals as to how they will see those plans through. Require them to share a way they practiced hospitality (and the results of it) during your next class period.

Final Inspection

1. List five things you would do to be hospitable to a guest in your home.
   A. _____
   B. _____
   C. _____
   D. _____
   E. _____

2. List five things you could do to be hospitable to someone not in your home.
   A. _____
   B. _____
   C. _____
   D. _____
   E. _____

3. List five examples of hospitality in Scripture.
   A. _____
   B. _____
   C. _____
   D. _____
   E. _____

4. As a member of your local assembly, list five ways you can be more hospitable to guests at your church.
   A. _____
   B. _____
   C. _____
   D. _____
   E. _____

5. Have you ever "played it forward" or "joyed" someone? If yes, what was the reaction? If not, why not?

   _____
   _____
   _____
   _____
   _____
   _____
   _____

Personal Study Notes

Lesson 9

Humanitarian Aid

Project Blueprints

After this lesson, students should be able to

- Define humanitarian aid
- Know what an NGO is
- Understand how to research NGOs
- Realize the need for humanitarian aid

In the Toolbox

Humanitarian aid: Humanitarian aid is material or logistical assistance provided for charitable purposes, typically in response to emergency crises, including natural as well as man-made disaster. The primary object of humanitarian aid is to save lives, alleviate suffering, and maintain human dignity. It may, therefore, be distinguished from developmental aid, which seeks to address the underlying socio-economic factors, which may have led to a crisis or emergency.

In His Word

Then the King will say to those on his right, "Come, you who are blessed by my Father; take your inheritance, the kingdom prepared for you since the creation of the world. For I was hungry and you gave me something to eat, I was thirsty, and you gave me something to drink, I was a stranger and you invited me in, I needed clothes and you clothed me, I was sick and you looked after me, I was in prison and you came to visit me." Then the righteous will answer him, "Lord, when did we see you hungry and feed you, or thirsty and give you something to drink? When did we see you a stranger and invite you in, or needing clothes and clothe you? When did we see you sick or in prison and go to visit you?" The King will reply, "Truly, I tell you, whatever you did for one of the least of these brothers and sisters of mine, you did for me." (Matthew 25:34–40, NIV)

Then Jesus said to his host, "When you give a luncheon or dinner, do not invite your friends, your brothers or sisters, your relatives, or your rich neighbors; if you do, they may invite you back and so you will be repaid. But when you give a banquet, invite the poor, the crippled, the lame, the blind, and you will be blessed. Although they cannot repay you, you will be repaid at the resurrection of the righteous." (Luke 14:12–14, NIV)

Is not this the kind of fasting I have chosen: to loose the chains of injustice and untie the cords of the yoke, to set the oppressed free and break every yoke? Is it not to share your food with the hungry and to provide the poor wanderer with shelter—when you see the naked to clothe them, and not to turn away from your own flesh and blood? (Isaiah 58:6–7, NIV)

In Their Shoes

Quesi heard the rumors in the village almost before they started. A well was coming; soon clean water would be available for all. He barely dared hope this might be true. For so long he and his family had done without clean water. The only water they were able to find to drink and use came from the muddy creek three miles from their home. Quesi made that trip every day. Three miles from his home to dip the muddy water of the same river people washed their clothes in, three miles back to his meager furnishings with the buckets of water he would carry. That water would last the family of six for about a day. Then he had to return to the creek to fetch more.

Well, Quesi sighed to himself sorrowfully, it was a family of five now. His little sister had succumbed to the ravages of typhoid fever. It could have been any number of waterborne diseases that ended her short life: cholera, guinea worm, dysentery—the list went on and on. Waterborne diseases are responsible for 3.4 million deaths every year, and Amefa would soon be just another number added to someone's charts for scientific calculation—if in fact anyone noticed she was gone at all.

Quesi noticed. Quesi noticed every single day as he trekked down to the creek to gather water his family desperately needed, knowing that same water might ultimately kill them all. Quesi had no way to describe the joy the news of a well brought to his spirit. He tried to squelch it. He barely dared hope it was true.

The rumors were at last confirmed, and Quesi could barely contain his joy. A well was being installed less than a mile from his house! He would have a place he could go to daily to provide clean water for him and his family—a much safer option and a MUCH less inconvenient walk. The whole trip would be done in a fourth of the time each day. He could hardly believe it!

He half walked, mostly ran, to the new well the first time he knew that it was open. The people in the compound that housed it were so nice and kind to everyone waiting in the long line for water. Quesi could hardly believe his eyes as the liquid poured into his buckets. It was absolutely clear of dirt, debris, or anything else that could cloud the precious water. The distance back to his home seemed like nothing at all as he carried life in his hands to give to his family. They would be free of disease now!

Quesi returned to the well day after day, retrieving the precious gift of life in his buckets seven times a week, and taking them home to his family. He made friendships along the way with the people he walked with and the people who worked at the compound that housed the well. Before long, he became curious about the joy on their faces and the kindness in their eyes. He began to ask questions about what made them so giving and loving, generous and kind.

In no time at all, Quesi, who came to the compound for water, was filled with living water from a well that would never run dry. He carried that same water home to his family, and to everyone he met along the way. His physical needs being met created space for his spiritual needs to be fulfilled.

The slogan of "Wells of Life UPCI" is "Providing Fresh and Living Water."

> Wells of Life Project is a United Pentecostal Church project dedicated to providing wells for locals in various communities inside the continent of Africa and the island nation of Haiti. These sources will provide sustenance and life for these locals and also provide an opportunity for us to reach the lost. (www.wellsoflifeupc.org.)

In Our Hands

Humanitarian aid is trendy right now. It's cool to buy an expensive pair of shoes that sends an equally expensive pair of shoes to someone in a country in need. It's popular to pour money into building wells for those without fresh water. Donating money to disease research centers is encouraged. It's fashionable to help those in need. And well it should be.

Even outside of the church, selfless giving is a popular idea and practice. According to Andrew Olsen Abstract, however, faith-based NGO's[1] constitute nearly 60 percent of all US-based foreign aid organizations. The majority of faith-based NGOs are Christian. *Forbes* reported in March 24, 2016, that three of the six largest US-based international aid charities are Christian, with combined revenue of $2.7 billion in 2014.

However, while these Christian-based aid organizations do reach out in the name of the Lord, they are not established or maintained for the express purpose of spreading the gospel. The president of the World Help organization, Vernon Brewer, said his group had not gone overseas to evangelize in tsunami-stricken areas. "First and foremost, our intention is not to evangelize but to show the love of Jesus Christ through our acts of compassion," Brewer told the *Washington Post*.

---

[1] Non-governmental organizations, commonly referred to as NGOs, are usually non-profit and sometimes international organizations independent of governments and international governmental organizations—though often funded by governments that are active in humanitarian, educational, health care, public policy, social, human rights, environmental, and other areas to effect changes according to their objectives.

"We are not using this open window of disaster to move in and set up a beachhead for evangelism. That's not the spirit of what we're trying to accomplish. We just want to show the genuine gospel."

Kenneth Chan reported for the *Christian Post* that the president of another aid organization, K. P. Yohannon, remarked on a return from Sri Lanka that efforts from his group and other Christian groups were not made in an attempt to trick or persuade others into his faith. "We give them all the material things, but at the same time, as the workers hearts hear the pain of these people—they're crying—they sit down with them and share the love of God and the hope in Jesus. To those who can read, they also give Scripture verses. That's all we do."

He said the objective is not to make converts in those dire circumstances. "As we go to these places, we are not going to give them food and clothes and medicine and housing to make them convert from their faith to Christianity," he says. "Jesus never did that; He went out doing good, it says in the Bible. He healed the sick; He fed the hungry; He cried with them."

Kenneth Chan also stated in his *Post* article that it is difficult to draw a line between what is acceptable and unacceptable behavior in foreign countries and that many religious charities—World Vision and Catholic Relief Services were named—prohibit mixing relief efforts with anything that might be viewed as proselytizing.

According to the dictionary, proselytizing is to "convert or attempt to convert (someone) from one religion, belief, or opinion to another." This is not the purpose of humanitarian aid. We do not reach hands out to the needy in order to persuade them to our point of view, but when we *do* reach hands out to them they are given a clear vision of the gospel of Christ, all it means, and its transformative power.

> Pure religion and undefiled before God and the Father is this, To visit the fatherless and widows in their affliction, and to keep himself unspotted from the world. (James 1:27)

When we practice humanitarian aid, we are practicing true religion. We are lifting God up in the truest sense of the word by "feeding Him when He was hungry" and "clothing Him when He was naked." What does Scripture say will happen when God is lifted up?

> And I, if I be lifted up from the earth, will draw all men unto me.
> (John 12:32)

We should not practice humanitarian aid in order to bring about our own agenda or to trick people into believing as we do. Nevertheless, by its very nature, it is true religion. By its very nature, it is the gospel. By its very nature, it is obedience. And by its very nature, it will draw all men to God.

In the Workshop

Wherever you are in the world, humanitarian aid likely reaches into your location. Assign your class the project of finding out what kinds of aid affect their local surroundings and to research the services provided, the source of funding, and the tenets of faith the founders hold. They might fill out a questionnaire sheet with the following questions:

- What is the name of the organization?
- What things do the organization provide?
- What is the organization's major source of funding?
- Where is the base of their general volunteer pool?
- What communities (or countries) does the organization provide aid to?
- Can locals volunteer to be a part?
- If yes, what role do locals play in the organization?

Final Inspection

1. Have you participated in giving humanitarian aid? If so, what kind of aid and what did you do? If not, why not?

_____
_____
_____

2. Do you agree that humanitarian aid should be free from evangelistic efforts? Why or why not?

3. How should the church respond to natural (divinely allowed) disasters?

4. Is giving humanitarian aid the same as preaching the gospel? Why or why not?

5. Should humanitarian aid be restricted to emergency crises, such as natural disasters, as opposed to ongoing welfare for the needy? Defend you answer.

Personal Study Notes

Lesson 10

Home Bible Studies

Project Blueprints

After this lesson, students should be able to

- Understand the concept and scriptural precedent for home Bible studies
- Know the requirements for a home Bible study
- Realize they can teach a home Bible study
- Identify sources for home Bible study material

In the Toolbox

Home Bible Study: In Christian communities, a Bible study is the analysis of the Bible by ordinary people as a personal religious or spiritual practice. Some denominations may call this devotion or devotional acts. A home Bible study is an event that takes place in someone's home, generally the home of the teacher but sometimes the home of the students.

In His Word

And let us consider one another to provoke unto love and to good works: not forsaking the assembling of ourselves together, as the manner of some is; but exhorting one another: and so much the more, as ye see the day approaching. (Hebrews 10:24–25)

> So continuing daily with one accord in the temple, and breaking bread from house to house, they ate their food with gladness and simplicity of heart, praising God and having favor with all the people. And the Lord added to the church daily those who were being saved. (Acts 2:46–47, NKJV)

In Their Shoes

Silas knocked on the door to Melanie's home, his Bible and his wife in tow. Melanie was a friend from Silas's place of business who had shown some interest in knowing more about the Lord and His Word. Silas had been praying for someone to share the gospel with, but now that the opportunity had presented itself, he found his heart was racing and his hands were clammy. His wife smiled and squeezed his arm. "You know this material backward and forword. You're going to do great."

Silas wished he could be as sure. But he knew that faith required action, so he steeled his nerves and mentally went over his main points one more time. The door opened to reveal a tall man with dark hair Silas had never seen before. This was not Melanie's fiancé, Rick. They had met several times at work parties, so Silas felt sure he would recognize him. Besides, Rick had blonde, almost white hair. Melanie often had made reference to it. The man in the doorway smiled and stuck out an affable hand for Silas and his wife, Annie, to shake.

"I'm Mark, Melanie's brother. Come in. She's expecting you." Silas and Annie soon learned that Mark was living with Melanie for the time being to help her cover the high cost of living in their town. They made their way into the living room where they found Melanie and Rick and seated themselves as Mark offered them something to drink. "I'm on the way out, but I'd be happy to grab you something before I leave. I'm assuming beer is not going to work for you," Mark said with a congenial twinkle in his eye and winning smile on his lips. Silas and Annie chuckled as they requested water, and as Mark went to get the refreshments, the group dove right into the Bible study.

Mark came back with the drinks, and he never left. He was utterly captivated by the things Silas had to say, more interested than Rick and Melanie. Mark never made it to his scheduled appointment that evening. He stayed right there in his own living room, learning all he could about the Lord, before asking if he might seek the gift of the Holy Ghost right there on the spot. When the group prayed together, Mark began to speak in other tongues, and when Silas and Annie left that evening, a new soul they had never met previously, and had not even known they were going to reach, was added to the roll in Heaven.

In Our Hands

After Acts 2:38, after the fire fell, after so many were added to their number that day—how did the church continue to grow? They went daily, with one accord, to the Temple to worship, and they broke bread from house to house. When they did that, the Lord added to their number daily those who were to be saved. All they had to do was worship the Lord, study the Word, and maintain open hearts and houses. Gathering to study the Word in houses was actually a common and well-documented practice in the New Testament.

Paul met a couple during his second missionary journey, for example, and here's what the Bible says about Aquila and Priscilla:

> Greet Priscilla and Aquila my helpers in Christ Jesus: who have for my life laid down their own necks: unto whom not only I give thanks, but also all the churches of the Gentiles. Likewise greet the church that is in their house. Salute my wellbeloved Epaenetus, who is the firstfruits of Achaia unto Christ. (Romans 16:3-5)

Nymphas, who lived in Laodicea, was also known to have gatherings in his home.

> Salute the brethren which are in Laodicea, and Nymphas, and the church which is in his house. And when this epistle is read among you, cause that it be read also in the church of the Laodiceans; and that ye likewise read the epistle from Laodicea. (Colossians 4:15-16)

It appears from Scripture that Philemon also hosted a house study: "And to our beloved Apphia, and Archippus our fellow soldier, and to the church in thy house" (Philemon 1-2)

You might be thinking it's great we've established through Scripture a record of people learning about the Lord and His Word in the houses of other believers. Nevertheless, it might sound a lot like hospitality as evangelism, a topic we have already covered. What makes this different from hospitality in general?

The hospitality lesson spoke of opening our homes to individuals in need of the love of the Lord and more information about Him, but that was where it stopped. It's not a method based on people coming to your home for the specific purpose of learning more about Scripture. Instead, it is a lifestyle of open love and concern, building relationship with those in your community and breaking bread together. It's making them welcome in your home whether they sign up for a Bible study or not. Hopefully, home gatherings of that sort will lead to a home Bible study, with people coming to your home for the sole purpose of studying the Word with you.

Aquila and Priscilla had such encounters in their homes, as we have already seen, and we read about them more specifically in Acts 18:24–28:

> And a certain Jew named Apollos, born at Alexandria, an eloquent man, and mighty in the scriptures, came to Ephesus. This man was instructed in the way of the Lord; and being fervent in the spirit, he spake and taught diligently the things of the Lord, knowing only the baptism of John. And he began to speak boldly in the synagogue: whom when Aquila and Priscilla had heard, they took him unto them, and expounded unto him the way of God more perfectly. And when he was disposed to pass into Achaia, the brethren wrote, exhorting the disciples to receive him: who, when he was come, helped them much which had believed through grace: for he mightily convinced the Jews, and that publickly, shewing by the scriptures that Jesus was Christ.

Because Aquila and Priscilla took Apollos under their wing and gave him further instruction in the gospel, he was able to "mightily convince the Jews that Jesus was the Christ." Their investment in one man changed the lives of many.

That is the power of a home Bible study. The best part of this is that anyone can teach a home Bible study. If you desire in your heart to learn more about God's Word and to lead others in doing the same, you can teach a Bible study. You don't even have to have a home. You can meet people for coffee; you can stand under a tree; or you can sit at a bus station. All that is required for a Bible study is you, a willing participant, and the Word of God.

So you've been listening to all of this, and you want to start a home Bible study. What is the ultimate goal? According to Howard Hendricks, the essential goal of a Bible study is twofold: (1) To present believers perfect in Christ, and (2) to equip them for ministry. The main objective as a teacher, he says, is not just the passing along of information, but change and the maturing of the individual being instructed.

With these two clear goals in mind for starting a Bible study in your home, you will also want to begin cultivating habits that will make you effective. Dave Earley lists eight of these habits:

1. Dream of leading a healthy, growing, multiplying group.
2. Pray for group members daily.
3. Invite new people to visit the group weekly.
4. Contact group members regularly.
5. Prepare for the group meeting.
6. Mentor an apprentice leader.
7. Plan group fellowship activities.
8. Be committed to personal growth.

With your goals in mind and an arsenal of healthy habits to cultivate, you will need material. The United Pentecostal Church International's Pentecostal Publishing House produces a lot of material, that might become available to you for purchase or by request (depending on your geographic location or what the church headquarters in your region has on hand.) Examples of studies available from PPH include:

Exploring God's Word
God's Word Made Plain
Into His Marvelous Light
How Do You Measure Up to the Word of God? by James Poitras
New Birth Experience by Michael G. Blankenship
What the Bible Says by Carlton L. Coon Sr.

Peter Krol also lists some helpful tips for preparing your own material on the website knowableword.com. Whether creating material from scratch or using someone else's material, these are good steps to follow:

1. **Depend on the Lord.**
   Prayer and leaning on the Lord should be a major part of your endeavor any time you seek to teach someone about the gospel or tenets of doctrine and faith. The Lord is in control, and the inspiration and unction of the Holy Spirit is needed to communicate His Word most effectively.

2. **Figure out what God has said.**
   Whatever you are seeking to communicate needs to be in line with the opinion of the Lord. Prayer and the careful study of Scripture will ensure this is the case.

3. **Allow the message to change you.**
   You should be passionate about what you are communicating, and you must never consider yourself above the message you are presenting to others. God's Word, His insight, His guidance—those are for you just as much as anyone you are communicating to.

4. **Decide how to lead your group toward what God has said.**
   Every method might not work for the person or group you are ministering to. You will need to pay close attention to their learning styles and to what they react to communicate most effectively.

5. **Consider the beginning.**
   For this particular sub point, Peter Krol stated:

   The most important part of the Bible study will be the first two minutes. You'll want to hook them and give them a reason to engage with the rest of the discussion. So think of a specific story to tell, or a specific question to ask, or a specific application to share. Your first words will set the tone for the rest of the study.

With God's Word in your hand and a passion for His people in your heart, you can change the lives of countless people right from your own home.

In the Workshop

Using some of the home Bible study material you have on hand, walk your students through the basics of giving a home Bible study through roleplay. Have each of them take a turn giving one to the class. Better yet—assign them to find a non-believer of their acquaintance who might be open to sitting through a Bible study they must give for their class assignment. You would be surprised how open some would be to helping out a friend in that way.

Final Inspection

1. Give scriptural references that show the early church used home Bible studies.

2. Describe a home Bible study. How would you facilitate a Bible study as the host?

3. What are the goals of a home Bible study?

4. What do home Bible studies require?

5. Where can you find material for a home Bible study?

   _____
   _____
   _____
   _____

Lesson 11

Knowing the Word

Project Blueprints

After this lesson, students should be able to

- Understand the importance of knowing Scripture
- Grasp the necessity of comprehending the doctrines of the Bible
- Realize the need to be able to defend their beliefs with Scripture
- Recognize the importance of memorizing Scripture
- Experience hiding the Word of God in their hearts

In the Toolbox

Scripture: The sacred writings of Christianity contained in the Bible.

The Bible (according to BBC Religions): The Christian Bible has two sections, the Old Testament and the New Testament. The Old Testament is the original Hebrew Bible, the sacred scriptures of the Jewish faith, written at different times between about 1200 and 165 BC. The New Testament books were written by Christians in the first century AD.

The Bible: "All scripture is given by inspiration of God, and is profitable for doctrine, for reproof, for correction, for instruction in righteousness: that the man of God may be perfect, thoroughly furnished unto all good works" (II Timothy 3:16–17).

In His Word

And take the helmet of salvation, and the sword of the Spirit, which is the word of God. (Ephesians 6:17)

But he answered and said, It is written, Man shall not live by bread alone, but by every word that proceedeth out of the mouth of God. (Matthew 4:4)

For whatsoever things were written aforetime were written for our learning, that we through patience and comfort of the scriptures might have hope. (Romans 15:4)

With my whole heart have I sought thee: O let me not wander from thy commandments. (Psalm 119:10–11)

Thy word have I hid in mine heart, that I might not sin against thee. (Psalm 119:11)

Keep my commandments, and live; and my law as the apple of thine eye. Bind them upon thy fingers, write them upon the table of thine heart. (Proverbs 7:2–3)

Your word is a lamp to my feet, and a light for my path. (Psalm 119:105, NKJV)

In Their Shoes

The room was full of pastors' children. When John had been asked to speak at this ministers' kids retreat, he had been given the topic "Do I Know What I Believe?" He had smiled the minute he saw that e-mail pop up in his inbox. He knew immediately that this would be challenging, effective, and fun. He opened the class simply by asking the teenagers the question found in the title: "Do You Know What You Believe?"

They were more than proud to proclaim they did. They were "One God, Apostolic, tongue talking, holy rolling, heaven bound, born again, believers" as the song they had all learned to sing at church camp said. They all knew what they believed. They were confident of this.

"Excellent!" John exclaimed. "What do we believe about the godhead?" They all believed that God is one.

"Amazing! Why?"

"What do you mean **why?**" they asked.

"**Why** do you believe that God is one? Where is that found in Scripture?"

The silence in the room was louder than a foghorn. Finally someone piped up in the back and said with pride, "Here O, Israel, the Lord our God is one Lord!"

"Good." John said. "Where is that found?"

No one knew. Several began rustling through their Bibles to find it. "However," John continued, "that says He's one Lord, not one God. Is that different? What about where it says, 'Let us make man in our image?' Anyone have an explanation for that?"

This question was met with blank stares and silence. "That's fine." John said, "Moving on, what about baptism. What name do we baptize in?"

They were more enthused about this question. "Jesus' name!"

"Great. Why?"

"Because THEN PETER SAID UNTO THEM . . . " the class erupted as they quoted Acts 2:38 in perfect and triumphant unison.

"Cool," said John. "But JESUS said, 'Go ye therefore and teach all nations baptizing them in the name of the Father, and of the Son, and of the Holy Ghost.' Why did that change?"

No one had a word to say. "Do any of you know any examples of any other places we are commanded to baptize in the name of Jesus?" Nothing. "Do any of you know instances in the Bible where people were baptized in the name of Jesus—or in the titles for that matter?" No one had a word to say.

John repeated this process over and over, asking question after question and playing devil's advocate each time an answer was given. "Why do we feel that way? How do we know that's what the Scripture meant? What's the reference for the verse you are quoting so I can see if that's what the Bible actually says."

The class stretched on and on. The longer it went, the more frustrated the students became. Some of them even got up and threatened to storm out. They were angry with the line of questioning, but they were also upset with themselves for not having better answers to combat it.

"It's not enough," John closed the hour out by saying, "to have a cursory knowledge of Scripture or a vague idea about the tenets of our faith. You have to know what you believe. You have to know why you believe it. And you have to be able to back it up when the time comes to share your faith. People are waiting on the good news of the gospel, which is found only in the Word. And if your words do not match up to the Word, you do yourselves, the gospel, our Savior, and the world we are trying to reach for Him a terrible injustice."

In Our Hands

It might seem obvious, but it is often overlooked. The Bible is the greatest weapon in our evangelism arsenal.

> For the word of God is quick, and powerful, and sharper than any twoedged sword, piercing even to the dividing asunder of soul and spirit, and of the joints and marrow, and is a discerner of the thoughts and intents of the heart. (Hebrews 4:12)

Knowing the Word is arguably the most important aspect of evangelism.

> But sanctify the Lord God in your hearts: and be ready always to give an answer to every man that asketh you a reason of the hope that is in you with meekness and fear. (I Peter 3:15)

We must first know what we believe before we can share it with anyone else. Not only that, but we must know it on more than a surface level. It's easy to feign knowledge or interest in something, or pretend you know what you're talking about, but when it comes down to it and a hungry soul is seeking truth and answers, more than a surface knowledge is needed.

It's like, for example, cooking. (This is an apt comparison considering, "Man shall not live by bread alone, but by every word that proceedeth out of the mouth of God" [Matthew 4:4].) Five minutes with a cookbook does not give you the knowledge needed to run a kitchen. In fact, even reading a cookbook for five minutes every day of your life would not give you the proper knowledge needed to express to someone else how bread is made or how to roast a chicken. People who cook well spend countless hours in the kitchen, interacting with their cookbooks and putting into practice the instructions found within them.

The same can be said with the Word of God. Ofttimes we think a cursory devotional every morning prepares us for witnessing to others. Checking off the "morning devotional" box is great, but the Word of God was created to be so much more to us than something we pause to read for a brief time in the morning. It's meant to be studied, interacted with, and is a living, breathing tool to aid in witnessing to others. When we interact with the Word of God on a more consistent basis, when we are constantly thinking about and practicing it, then we are better able to do all that is written in it and instruct others in doing the same.

> This book of the law shall not depart out of thy mouth; but thou shalt meditate therein day and night, that thou mayest observe to do according to all that is written therein: for then thou shalt make thy way prosperous, and then thou shalt have good success. (Joshua 1:8)

The Bible is an exceptional book. There is no other book like it. It is *inerrant:* incapable of being wrong. It is *infallible:* never failing, or always effective. It is *sufficient:* enough, adequate. It is *authoritative:* able to be trusted as accurate or true, reliable. It is *alive:* living, not dead. You can read Scripture over and over again, discovering something new each time, because it is living. You would not find an error in it. You would not find one teaching to be false, or one promise to be void.

Charles F. Stanley lists six things the Word does that no other book can do.

1. It leads us to salvation. (John 3:16; Romans 10:9; I Peter 1:23).
2. It guides our steps. (Psalm 119:105)
3. It directs us to wisdom. (Psalm 119:130)
4. It lifts our burden. (Psalm 119:28)
5. It brings joy. (Psalm 119:111)
6. It gives peace. (Psalm 119:165; John 14:27)

This truly is a book like none other. It brings life, because it is alive. It is a powerful weapon. When we interact with it, when we study it, when we open our mouths and speak it and share it with others, it truly changes lives.

In the Workshop

The following paragraphs are the basic tenets of belief found on the website of the United Pentecostal Church International. They are the core doctrines of our faith. You can interact with your class in many ways using these. You could question them about the basic points, requiring them to give Scripture to back up their beliefs, for example. You might print off (or write on notecards) the belief statements and write the verses on separate notecards, so they have to be matched up to the appropriate phrases. Whatever you do, scriptural knowledge will be tested, and the classroom will be challenged to know what they believe.

> The Bible is the infallible Word of God and the authority for salvation and Christian living.
>
> There is one God, who has revealed Himself as our Father, in His Son Jesus Christ, and as the Holy Spirit. Jesus Christ is God manifested in flesh. He is both God and man.
>
> Everyone has sinned and needs salvation. Salvation comes by grace through faith based on the atoning sacrifice of Jesus Christ.
>
> The saving gospel is the good news that Jesus died for our sins, was buried, and rose again. We obey the gospel by repentance (death to sin), water baptism in the name of Jesus Christ (burial), and the baptism of the Holy Spirit with the initial sign of speaking in tongues as the Spirit gives the utterance (resurrection).
>
> As Christians we are to love God and others. We should live a holy life inwardly and outwardly, and worship God joyfully. The supernatural gifts of the Spirit, including healing, are for the church today.

Jesus Christ is coming again to catch away His church. In the end will be the final resurrection and the final judgment. The righteous will inherit eternal life, and the unrighteous eternal death. (https://www.upci.org/about/our-beliefs)

II Timothy 3:5-17	Deuteronomy 6:4	Ephesians 4:4-6
Colossian 2:9	I Timothy 3:16	Romans 3:23-25
Romans 6:23	Ephesians 2:8-9	II Thessalonians 1:8
I Peter 4:17	I Corinthians 15:1-4	Acts 2:4
Romans 6:3-4	Mark 12:28-31	II Corinthians 7:1
Hebrews 12:14	I Corinthians 12:8-10	I Thessalonians 4:16-17
Revelation 20:11-15		

Final Inspection

1. Do you agree with John that one needs to know what he or she believes? If yes, why? If no, why not?

   _____
   _____
   _____
   _____

2. Using Scripture, explain the oneness of God.

   _____
   _____
   _____
   _____
   _____
   _____
   _____
   _____

3. Using Scripture, explain why we baptize in Jesus' name.

   _____
   _____
   _____
   _____
   _____
   _____
   _____

4. What's the difference between showing hospitality and teaching a home Bible study?

   _____
   _____
   _____
   _____

5. List 3 different steps or approaches you might take to initiate a home Bible study.
   A. _____
   _____

   B. _____
   _____

   C. _____
   _____

Lesson 12

Community Outreach

Project Blueprints

After this lesson, students should be able to

- Know the scriptural basis for community outreach
- Recognize needs in the community that churches can help relieve
- Plan a community outreach program to address needs in the neighborhood
- Organize an emergency plan in case of natural disaster
- Become personally involved in a community outreach program

In the Toolbox

Community: A group of people living in the same place or having a particular characteristic in common; a feeling of fellowship with others, as a result of sharing common attitudes, interests, and goals.

In His Word

But ye shall receive power, after that the Holy Ghost is come upon you: and ye shall be witnesses unto me both in Jerusalem, and in all Judaea, and in Samaria, and unto the uttermost part of the earth. (Acts 1:8)

How good and pleasant it is when God's people live together in unity! (Psalm 133:1, NIV)

Live in harmony with one another. Do not be proud, but be willing to associate with people of low position. Do not be conceited. (Romans 12:16, NIV)

In Their Shoes

Rolando had not been so excited in a long time. The man the boys had been observing playing soccer with his friends in the park had just invited Rolando and all his buddies to join the game. This man had some moves—we're talking World Cup material. Rolando and his friends would often watch the older boys playing their weekly soccer games, and some of the man's friends were not bad, but he really stood out from the rest of them with impressive skill and fancy footwork. Now, the boys had been honored by being asked by the adults if they would like to play.

Rolando couldn't believe it, because he knew their own level of skill would slow the men's game down. He knew it all too well; his father had often shooed him away when he was in the midst of a game with his buddies—that is, until his dad had left for good. This man though, in spite of the inconvenience adding young players to the game would cause, was welcoming the boys into this treasured circle. Rolando would now be a part of what he had only been able to watch from afar.

Week after week passed, and the men met the boys on the circle field every single Tuesday. Rolando learned the man's name was Matt. He took extra time after the game to teach the boys his special moves and tricks, showing unending patience with them as they fumbled the ball repeatedly.

Soon Matt knew all about the things the boys went going through: how things were at home and in their relationships. He was a sympathetic listener and gave amazing advice. Soccer games became dinners at Matt's house, home cooked by his beautiful wife, and long conversations about careers and goals and people they both knew.

Soon the boys weren't just playing soccer and going to dinner. They were going to church as well. They loved Matt's church and the way they felt when they were worshiping with the church family. By the time Matt had children, Rolando was their Sunday school teacher. And as soon as the boys got old enough to play, Rolando met his Sunday school students every single Tuesday to play soccer.

In Our Hands

> May the God who gives endurance and encouragement give you the same attitude of mind toward each other that Christ Jesus had. (Romans 15:5, NIV)

Jesus could constantly be found where the people were. He didn't even seem to care much what *kind* of people they were. He could be found ministering on hillsides, making wine at weddings, having dinner with the tax collectors and people of ill repute, and allowing little children to come to Him and take up His time. He was amazing at working a crowd and walking with the people. In fact, when He was just a young man, His parents lost Him at a gathering, only to find Him days later explaining Scripture to religious leaders in the Temple.

Jesus knew what it meant to be a part of a community. Ministering directly to the community has always been a part of His plan for us as well. When believers were told they would receive power after the Holy Ghost had come upon them, the very first place they were meant to be witnesses was in Jerusalem. Yes, the circle widened into Judaea, then Samaria, and finally into the uttermost part of the earth. Nevertheless, it started right in the home region of those who received the Spirit, as believers actively reached out into their own communities.

When Hurricane Harvey hit Houston, Texas, in 2017, Pentecostal churches—and churches of every other denomination—immediately responded. Supplies were gathered; help was sent. Church leaders went out in boats to rescue people from their homes. They set up cots in local churches so people could sleep there..

Over 100,000 people lost their homes in the flooding caused by the hurricane, and they needed a place to go. The community needed direct help, so the church responded directly. They didn't do it for fame or fortune; they didn't do it because they wanted to add to their numbers for their next quarterly report. They did it because it was the right thing to do.

Because of that, countless lives were saved, families were helped, the gospel was delivered, and the president of the United States, Donald Trump, visited one of our churches. The church was not seeking the attention of the president, but his attention was caught because people were serving their community. Out of love. Just because it was the right thing to do. Just because "they had the same attitude and mind toward each other that Christ had."

Rob Toal writes about Missio Dei, a church in Chicago that has multiple congregations. Each campus of this church attempts to bring the gospel to light by being actively involved in their community. The leadership is encouraged to build relationship with local city leaders, serve on boards in the community, or join the Parent Teacher Association at their children's school. Missional groups are gathered by neighborhood. They take care of refugee families. They join in city farming. They attend and are active in local events.

They hold events called "You Are Loved," where they offer coffee to people heading to work and take free photographs for families who would not be able to afford professional photos. The lead pastor of these church campuses, Josh Taylor, says, "We're not trying to build a mega-church across ZIP codes. We're going for the presence of Christ in a specific neighborhood. With no strings attached, we're seeking to live out the question, 'How can we be a blessing to this community?'"

Toal references another church, Peace of Christ Church in Westmont, Illinois, which teaches the importance of presence and encourages people to be active in their communities. David Fitch, the pastor of that church, says, "Pray for that space [the community you seek to witness to] and become sensitive to what God is doing."

All over the world, in so many ways, churches can reach out to their communities A simple Google search provides a wealth of ideas. A church could find local law enforcement officers, construction workers, telephone operators, mail carriers, emergency response teams and give them free lunches. They could provide meals, cookies, gift baskets, or other nice treats to the teachers at a local school. Free candy or gum could be handed out to parents and children attending a parade or other large event, or even just walking around the market or shopping center.

Widows without a husband to take care of maintenance on their houses or cleaning up their yards could be served. If the community has a local fair, art exhibit, or craft show, experienced church members could create things and participate with a booth. Free ice water could be handed out at busy traffic intersections, shopping centers, or parks. A church could locate children without parents and bless them with free food, games, and a school supply or clothes giveaway. People who are working in fields or other forms of manual labor could be blessed with sweets, or even full meals packed in sacks. Nicely packaged food could also be distributed at bus stops and transit stations. Rides could be offered to those who cannot get to church by themselves. Christians can be a blessing in their communities in so many ways, and these ways are not limited by culture or country — no matter where you are, you can find a way to reach out to those in your area.

My local church is beginning to start interest-based small groups. What this means is that you find people with common interests: who all like to read, or sew, or fish, or do bead crafting — it could be anything — and the people in the church who like to do those things get together once a week or twice a month and they participate in those activities together.

Let's say you are in a group of people who knit things out of yarn. Then, when you meet someone at the craft store who also knits things, you can invite them to your interest group. Before you know it, a stranger has been surrounded by godly influences, and you are given multiple opportunities to share the gospel with someone who needs it.

The possibilities are endless. All you have to do is become involved in your community, and the Lord will open doors.

In the Workshop

Instruct your students to draft a community outreach plan as a class. Include practical ways for your location and country so they can reach into the community around them. It doesn't have to — nor should it — look like community outreach would look in North America. Nevertheless, the basic principles can be applied to specific needs for specific areas. The plan should be comprehensive, actionable, and contain multiple steps.

Final Inspection

1. List five needs in your neighborhood that could be addressed by community outreach.
   A. _____
   B. _____
   C. _____
   D. _____
   E. _____

2. What could you personally do to help with need B listed above?
   _____
   _____
   _____
   _____

3. What would you do to solicit help for need C?
   _____
   _____
   _____
   _____

4. What is the scriptural basis for community outreach?
   _____
   _____
   _____
   _____

5. Should community outreach be restricted to emergency situations? If yes, why? If no, why not?

_____
_____
_____
_____
_____
_____
_____
_____

Personal Study Notes

Lesson 13

Financial Giving

Project Blueprints

After this lesson, students should be able to

- Show the scriptural basis for giving
- Realize the need to help various ministries and ministers
- Formulate a plan to invest in someone else's ministry
- Devise a method to solicit funds for their own ministry

In the Toolbox

Giving: Freely transfer the possession of (something) to (someone); hand over to; cause or allow (someone or something) to have (something, especially something abstract); provide or supply with.

In His Word

Bring the whole tithe into the storehouse, that there may be food in my house. Test me in this," says the LORD Almighty, "and see if I will not throw open the floodgates of heaven and pour out so much blessing that there will not be room enough to store it. (Malachi 3:10, NIV)

In everything I did, I showed you that by this kind of hard work we must help the weak, remembering the words the Lord Jesus himself said: "It is more blessed to give than to receive." (Acts 20:35, NIV)

Now he who supplies seed to the sower and bread for food will also supply and increase your store of seed and will enlarge the harvest of your righteousness. (II Corinthians 9:10, NIV)

Heal the sick, raise the dead, cleanse those who have leprosy, drive out demons. Freely you have received; freely give. (Matthew 10:8, NIV)

In Their Shoes

John opened the letter he had received to read the following words:

Hi.

I don't believe in myself very much. I know that must seem a strange way to start something like this, but I must tell you the story of this journey and this is how it begins:

> I don't believe in myself very much. That's why the strong pull that I've felt towards missions the majority of my life has often been pushed aside or swept under the rug. After all, who am I to go anywhere, do anything, or teach anyone? It was inescapable regardless. Try to avoid it as I might, the pull was persistent; the calling was consistent. My heart was forever loving people I have never met; my head forever thinking of ways to reach them. I wouldn't go though. I would stay, I would serve. I would give, but I wouldn't go. Who am I to go anywhere, do anything, or teach anyone?

> In 2016 I attended the Global ConNEXTions gathering in St. Louis. Every speaker, every song, every interactive experience seemed to speak to me specifically, call to me as an individual. The last day of the conference, sitting at a round table discussion, I was

asked what I wanted to do and where I wanted to go. It just popped out of my mouth: "I want to take a missions trip to Scotland."

In that moment I realized that is exactly what I want to do. The Great Commission of a Man who sacrificed His broken body states that we must go into all nations preaching the gospel. When He says that, He means me. When He says we are a chosen generation and a royal priesthood, He means me. When He says that His gifts and His calling are without repentance, He means the gifts and the calling that He has given to me. He does not call only the qualified, but He also qualifies the called.

I realize now that I can go anywhere, do anything, and teach anyone because when He says all things can be done through His strength, He is talking about me. I may not believe in myself very much, but He believes in me enough to stake His life on it, to stake His life right to a cross.

The Next Steps program this year just so happens to be in Scotland, the very place I felt the Lord calling me to go. The three-week, intensive training program will teach me about other cultures, introduce me to missionary practices, and prepare me to minister to the people of Europe before I and a team of other young people spend five more weeks witnessing, teaching, and extending God's hand of grace to His people on the other side of the pond.

It is my hope that my background in home missions work, my experience as part of a family who offered a home to troubled foster children, and my education in the field of teaching will be put to good use on foreign soil. I'm scared, I'm nervous, I'm excited, and primarily I'm convinced. I'm convinced that this is God's plan for my life and while I may not deserve such an honor, and could never earn it on my own merit, He will use me as an extension of His hands and heart this summer.

There is no way that I would ever be able to accomplish any of this without His help, or yours. I've been setting aside most of each paycheck, participating in craft shows, and selling home-made desserts in order to save money for this trip, but I still need to raise $6,500 by the beginning of May. If I could find sixty-five people who would give me one hundred dollars each, this would be completely taken care of. Whether through financial giving or prayer your support of this trip is indispensable.

Thank you for taking the time to read this letter and considering giving me your support. I will be a reputable and effective extension of your giving in Scotland this summer, believing in the One who believes in me, and strengthened by knowing you believe in me too.

With much love,

Aria

John did believe in Aria. He hadn't seen her in years, but her heart for souls was the most memorable thing about her. It had been visible and vibrant all during their time at school together. John also believed in the ability money had to put feet on the gospel. When John folded the letter and went to get his checkbook that day, he could not possibly know all the lives he would impact, all the souls who would receive witness of God's love and grace, but he had an inkling.

In Our Hands

It has often been said, "Some give by going and others go by giving." We cannot discuss methods of evangelism without discussing financial giving. Giving has been an important method of evangelism since the start of the church. Paul included a thank-you note in his letter to the Philippians, expressing his gratitude for their financial support of his ministry.

> Notwithstanding ye have well done, that ye did communicate with my affliction. Now ye Philippians know also, that in the beginning of the gospel, when I departed from Macedonia, no church communicated with me as concerning giving and receiving, but ye only. For even in Thessalonica ye sent once and again unto my necessity. Not because I desire a gift: but I desire fruit that may

abound to your account. But I have all, and abound: I am full, having received of Epaphroditus the things which were sent from you, an odour of a sweet smell, a sacrifice acceptable, wellpleasing to God. But my God shall supply all your need according to his riches in glory by Christ Jesus. (Philippians 4:14-19)

He also clearly outlines the principle of giving to support those who are going forth with the gospel in his letter to the Corinthians.

Do we not have the right to have food and drink when we are working for the Lord? Do we not have the right to take a Christian wife along with us? The other missionaries do. The Lord's brothers do and Peter does. Are Barnabas and I the only ones who should keep working for a living so we can preach? Have you ever heard of a soldier who goes to war and pays for what he needs himself? Have you ever heard of a man planting a field of grapes and not eating some of the fruit? Have you ever heard of a farmer who feeds cattle and does not drink some of the milk? These things are not just what men think are right to do. God's Law speaks about this. God gave Moses the Law. It says, "When the cow is made to walk on the grain to break it open, do not stop it from eating some." Does God care about the cow? Did not God speak about this because of us. For sure, this was written for us. The man who gets the fields ready and the man who gathers in the grain should expect some of the grain. We have planted God's Word among you. Is it too much to expect you to give us what we need to live each day? (I Corinthians 9:4-11, NLV)

Jesus Himself left us with a heavy final charge in Mathew 28:18-20. We are called and commanded to "go ye therefore and preach to all nations." We know it is the heart of God above all else that the lost be saved and the center of our purpose as Christians is to fuel that commandment with our lives.

People need a preacher. "How then shall they call on Him in whom they have not believed? and how shall they believe in Him of whom they have not heard? and how shall they hear without a preacher? And how shall they preach unless they are sent?" (Romans 10:14-15) People must believe on the Lord to be saved. They cannot believe if they have not heard. They cannot hear without a preacher. And a preacher, especially one who is dedicating his life to the ministry of the gospel full time, must be "sent" through the financial aid of God's people.

The will of the Lord is to establish His kingdom here on earth. When we pray, we are encouraged to pray, "Your kingdom come, your will be done, on earth as it is in heaven" (Matthew 6:10, NIV). In addition to praying for His kingdom to be established, we are also admonished to seek His kingdom first. (See Matthew 6:33.) Our lives are full of work and toil but are not to be dedicated toward accumulating earthly acclaim or gain. We are called to "lay up for ourselves treasures in heaven, where neither moth nor rust doth corrupt, and where thieves do not break through nor steal" (Matthew 6:20). You would be hard pressed to find a better way to do that than to directly invest your treasure straight into the kingdom of God. We must all bring souls into the Kingdom one way or the other.

> "I have planted, Apollos watered; but God gave the increase. So then neither is he that planteth anything, neither he that watereth; but God that giveth the increase. Now he that planteth and he that watereth are one: and every man shall receive his own reward according to his own labour." (I Corinthians 3:6–8)

We are all called to play some role (or even multiple roles) in the process of soulwinning. We must tell others about Jesus. We must stand by each other's side and support new converts in the process of growing in the knowledge of the Lord and His kingdom. We must encourage each other, provoking each other unto good works.

We are called to go at some level. We are called to give at some level. It's all about the Kingdom in the end. It's all about the souls, and if we did everything we possibly could do to reach them by using every one of our possible resources. We need never worry we will come up short in the end, or spend all our resources, leaving nothing with which to provide for ourselves. "For God is not unjust so as to overlook your work and the love that you have shown for his name in serving the saints, as you still do." (Hebrews 6:10, ESV)

We can boldly go forward, expending all our resources in taking care of God's people, knowing full well that God takes care of His people too.

In the Workshop

Encourage your class to find some way to "go by giving" this week. Have them report of where they have financially invested in the Kingdom (specifically by financially furthering some evangelistic effort or another) by the next class period.

Final Inspection

1. Cite three scriptural references showing God has ordained giving.
   A. _____
   B. _____
   C. _____

2. How did Paul finance his missionary journeys?
   _____
   _____
   _____
   _____

3. What is the UPCI's funding program for its global missionaries?
   _____
   _____
   _____
   _____

4. How can short-term missionaries raise their support?
   _____
   _____
   _____
   _____

5. Plan a budget for a short-term missionary who is coming to your country for six months.

   Food   _____
   Housing   _____
   Travel   _____
   _____   _____
   _____   _____
   _____   _____
   _____   _____
   _____   _____
   _____   _____

Lesson 14

The Evangelist

Project Blueprints

After this lesson, students should be able to

- List the fivefold ministry
- Describe the work of an evangelist
- Recognize the characteristics needed to be an evangelist
- Be willing to be an evangelist
- Know how to support an evangelist's ministry

In the Toolbox

Evangelist: A person who seeks to convert others to the Christian faith, especially by public preaching

In His Word

The word of the LORD came unto Jonah the son of Amittai saying, Arise, go to Nineveh the great city, and cry against it; for their wickedness is come up before me. (Jonah 1:1–2)

These twelve Jesus sent out after instructing them: "Do not go in the way of the Gentiles, and do not enter any city of the Samaritans; but rather go to the lost sheep of the house of Israel. And as you go, preach, saying, 'The kingdom of heaven is at hand.'" (Matthew 10:5-7, NASB)

And He said to them, "Take nothing for your journey, neither a staff, nor a bag, nor bread, nor money; and do not even have two tunics apiece. Whatever house you enter, stay there until you leave that city. And as for those who do not receive you, as you go out from that city, shake the dust off your feet as a testimony against them." (Luke 9:3-5, NASB)

The Spirit of the Lord GOD is upon me, because the LORD has anointed me to bring good news to the afflicted; He has sent me to bind up the brokenhearted, to proclaim liberty to captives and freedom to prisoners; to proclaim the favorable year of the LORD and the day of vengeance of our God; to comfort all who mourn, to grant those who mourn in Zion, giving them a garland instead of ashes, the oil of gladness instead of mourning, the mantle of praise instead of a spirit of fainting. So they will be called oaks of righteousness, the planting of the LORD, that He may be glorified. (Isaiah 61:1-3, NASB)

For the time will come when they will not endure sound doctrine; but wanting to have their ears tickled, they will accumulate for themselves teachers in accordance to their own desires, and will turn away their ears from the truth and will turn aside to myths. But you, be sober in all things, endure hardship, do the work of an evangelist, fulfill your ministry. (II Timothy 4:3-5, NASB)

Until I come, give attention to the public reading of Scripture, to exhortation and teaching. (I Timothy 4:13, NASB)

How then will they call on Him in whom they have not believed? How will they believe in Him whom they have not heard? And how will they hear without a preacher? How will they preach unless they are sent? Just as it is written, "HOW BEAUTIFUL ARE THE FEET OF THOSE WHO BRING GOOD NEWS OF GOOD THINGS!" (Romans 10:14-15, NASB)

In Their Shoes

Jack sat in the service, listening to the evangelist preaching. He admired this man so much. Faith-building story after story fell from the evangelist's lips as he told of time after time God had used him to minister to his family, strangers on the bus, or people in the grocery store. He told stories of people receiving their healing in town squares, the Holy Ghost in living rooms, being baptized in inflatable pools on back porches. People were being reached by this man wherever he went, whatever he did. He was blessed beyond measure and clearly anointed.

Jack longed to be just like that man. He longed to be a witness for Jesus and a light to his family. He just didn't know how. When the altar call was given, Jack found a quiet corner to pray in. He buried his face in his hands and poured out his heart to God. He told Him he was willing and asked Him to make Him a servant—a person who could spread the good news of the gospel far and abroad.

He didn't know where to begin, but he was ready to start. He knew he didn't have the "gift of evangelism." People were not really drawn to him in public settings, and he had never laid hands on anyone in a restaurant or at the market. However, he so desperately wanted to make a difference for God.

Jack felt firm hands on his head as he heard the voice of the evangelist begin to speak. "Lord, You have called and anointed this man. You will help him be a witness to the nations. A willing heart is all you need. This willing heart is what you will use." Jack was overcome with emotion. He knew now that even if he didn't have all the skills he wanted, God would supply all that he needed.

In Our Hands

Popular theology these days discusses the "gift of evangelism." Is there any such thing? Matt Queen supposes not when he expounds upon the success of the early church.

> In reality mirroring fantasy, Jesus assembled an unlikely group consisting of fishermen, a tax collector, and a Zealot in an assault on the ruler of this world (John 12:31) by proclaiming the Gospel of the Kingdom of God. What was the secret of their success? Those who

heard them preach perceived them as untrained and uneducated men (Acts 4:13a). How, then, did those who preached the Gospel "turn the world upside down" (Acts 17:6, ESV)? They did it through their Gospel preaching due to time spent with Jesus (Acts 4:13b), because they had received the Holy Spirit (Acts 2:4, 18).

We know that "He gave some as apostles, and some as prophets, and some as evangelists, and some as pastors and teachers, for the equipping of the saints for the work of service, to the building up of the body of Christ" (Ephesians 4:11-12, NASB), so some are more naturally gifted in the work of witnessing to the lost. However, no evidence suggests one must have the "gift of evangelism" before witnessing to the lost and dying world. In fact, the Lord has been calling whoever He wants, to go wherever He wants, whenever He wants, since the beginning of time, and He surely equips those He calls.

We are *all* called to look beyond ourselves, put away selfish ambition, and reach out into the world around us. We are *all* called to take up our cross and follow Him. *All* are called to be salt and light. How best do we do that? What makes a good evangelist? Are we all capable of becoming one?

Thom S. Rainer comments on the "Qualities of Highly Evangelistic Christians." Reading his writing, I saw that evangelists are surely in touch with God. They know He is the one who draws men to Him and are completely reliant upon Him and His saving and drawing power through prayer. They have a personal belief construct that stirs them on to evangelism. They have wholehearted faith in the gospel of Jesus Christ and are deeply convicted that He is the only way a soul can be saved from the fiery flames of Hell.

Evangelists read their Bible. They are quick to sense God's heart and see the need of His people because of time they spend studying His Word and reading about His plans. They have God's heart for His people. They mourn for those who don't know what it's like to walk with Jesus, and they love the world He came to save. They want everyone to know Jesus and walk with Him. They cultivate love for the people right where they are. They spend time with people in their towns and communities, interacting with them and serving them because they want to be an example of Christ's love to those around them. They go with God's feet, help with His hands, and love with His heart.

Evangelists witness intentionally. They ask the Lord to send them people to witness to, to create moments for them to speak of His Word and His goodness. They seek times where they can tell someone about Jesus and view what we might look at as coincidence as divine appointments set by God.

Does that sound like something you could do? Can you stay in touch with God? Can you foster a personal belief construct that might stir you on to evangelism? Do you have wholehearted faith in the gospel of Jesus Christ? Are you aware He is the only way a soul can be saved? Do you read your Bible? Do you have God's heart for His people? Do you want everyone to know Jesus and walk with Him? Can you cultivate a love for the people around you? Then you can be an evangelist. Through the power of God's Word and with His help, you could win many souls to the Lord.

Al Maxey lists some important evangelistic qualities we should all cultivate:

1. Having a good reputation (Acts 6:3)
2. Living as an example to/of those who believe (I Timothy 4:12; Titus 2:7)
3. Staying full of the Spirit (Acts 6:3)
4. Developing instead of neglecting the spiritual gifts within us (I Timothy 4:14; II Timothy 1:6)
5. Pursuing personal growth and progress (I Timothy 4:15)
6. Maintaining personal purity (I Timothy 5:22)
7. Fleeing from youthful lusts and pursuing righteousness (I Timothy 6:11; II Timothy 2:22)
8. Being non-materialistic (I Timothy 6:7-11)
9. Avoiding and shunning controversies (I Timothy 4:7; 6:20; II Timothy 2:16, 22-23; Titus 3:9)
10. Being constantly nourished by study of the Word and sound doctrine (I Timothy 4:6), thus gaining a deep understanding of what He teaches (I Timothy 1:6-7; 4:16; II Timothy 2:15; 3:14-15)
11. Staying vigilant (I Timothy 6:20; II Timothy 1:13-14)
12. Maintaining a sincere faith and good conscience (I Timothy 1:19; II Timothy 1:5)
13. Being unashamed of the gospel, nor put to shame by our inaccurate handling of it (II Timothy 1:8; 2:15)
14. Remaining sober or circumspect in all things (II Timothy 4:5)
15. Avoiding a cowardly or timid spirit (II Timothy 1:7)

16. Remaining full of wisdom/knowledge/enlightenment (Acts 6:3)
17. Choosing to be self-disciplined (I Timothy 4:7, 16)
18. Staying devoted to the work/ministry (I Timothy 4:15–16; II Timothy 2:15)
19. Having a willingness to endure hardship, suffering, and persecution (II Timothy1:8; 2:3; 4:5)
20. Enduring patiently wrongs and injuries done to us by others (II Timothy 2:24)
21. Being kind to all (II Timothy 2:24)
22. Remaining unbiased and impartial (I Timothy 5:21)

We might not all naturally excel in all these areas, but we can improve and develop ourselves through prayer and reading of the Word, by stepping outside of our comfort zones and practicing evangelistic methods. Damien T. Garofalo points to compassion, boldness, and wisdom as the most important qualities of an evangelist. There's a story found in the Book of Jonah about a man named, well, Jonah, whom the Lord chose to call as an evangelist.

> The word of the LORD came to Jonah son of Amittai: "Go to the great city of Nineveh and preach against it, because its wickedness has come up before me." (Jonah 1:1–2, NIV)

Jonah was not very bold.

> [He] ran away from the LORD and headed for Tarshish. (Jonah 1:3, NIV)

Jonah was not very wise.

> But God said to Jonah, "Is it right for you to be angry about the plant?" "It is," he said. "And I'm so angry I wish I were dead." (Jonah 4:9, NIV)

Jonah was definitely not very compassionate.

> But the LORD said, "You have been concerned about this plant, though you did not tend it or make it grow. It sprang up overnight and died overnight. And should I not have concern for the great city

of Nineveh, in which there are more than a hundred and twenty thousand people who cannot tell their right hand from their left — and also many animals?" (Jonah 4:10–11, NIV)

Still, God was able to use Jonah for His glory and His fame, to save the people of Nineveh from certain death. Because of this, I believe that above all else, the most important characteristic of an evangelist is just willingness. We are all imperfect people who have the privilege of being chosen by God. Are you willing to work for Him? Are you willing to work on your own character and your own heart? Are you willing to go? Willing to witness? I hope you're willing. He's waiting to use you.

In the Workshop

Challenge your class to thoughtfully pray and peruse the evangelistic qualities in this lesson, noting areas in which they are lacking. Instruct them to share with their classmates these areas in which they most need help and to uplift one another in prayer.

Final Inspection

1. According to Ephesians 4:11–12, what is the fivefold ministry?
    A. _____
    B. _____
    C. _____
    D. _____
    E. _____

2. What is the work of an evangelist?
    _____
    _____
    _____
    _____

3. List five characteristics an evangelist needs.
    A. _____
    B. _____
    C. _____
    D. _____
    E. _____

4. List five men in Scripture who were evangelists. Support your choices with scriptural references.
    A. _____
    B. _____
    C. _____
    D. _____
    E. _____

5. If God called you to be an evangelist, how would you prepare?
    _____
    _____
    _____
    _____
    _____

Lesson 15

Evangelistic Sermons

Project Blueprints

After this lesson, students should be able to

- Recognize the decline of evangelistic preaching
- Understand the need for evangelistic preaching
- Grasp the goal of evangelistic preaching
- Know how to craft an evangelistic sermon
- Experience preaching an evangelistic sermon

In the Toolbox

Evangelistic preaching: a type of preaching that expounds on God's Word with the primary aim of the salvation of lost souls. It is becoming increasingly rare today.

In His Word

He said to them, "Go into all the world and preach the gospel to all creation." (Mark 16:15, NIV)

And my message and my preaching were not in persuasive words of wisdom, but in demonstration of the Spirit and of power, so that your faith would not rest on the wisdom of men, but on the power of God. (I Corinthians 2:4–5, NASB)

But He said to them, "I must preach the kingdom of God to the other cities also, for I was sent for this purpose." (Luke 4:43, NASB)

He said to them, "Let us go somewhere else to the towns nearby, so that I may preach there also; for that is what I came for." (Mark 1:38, NASB)

But just as we have been approved by God to be entrusted with the gospel, so we speak, not as pleasing men, but God who examines our hearts. (I Thessalonians 2:4, NASB)

Preach the word; be ready in season and out of season; reprove, rebuke, exhort, with great patience and instruction. (II Timothy 4:2, NASB)

Let not many of you become teachers, my brethren, knowing that as such we will incur a stricter judgment. (James 3:1, NASB)

In Their Shoes

Pastor Sam struggled with the thought of preaching evangelistic sermons. The members of the congregation knew the need of repentance, baptism in Jesus' name, and receiving the Holy Ghost. They were already saved, pulled out of the raging river and into the boat. Sam almost felt that preaching to them about salvation was like handing life jackets to people walking on solid ground.

Pastor Sam's mother disagreed with him. She said that people always need a refresher course, always need to be edified by the gospel message, and can never hear enough times the way to Heaven.

So Sam prepared an evangelistic sermon. He preached it to his faithful congregation who already knew all there was to discover about salvation—or so he thought. Member after member came up to Sam after church and thanked him for preaching that sermon. They thanked him because they had brought family members or friends with them, and those people had heard the gospel message articulated fully. They thanked him because they had been sitting on the pew, slowly dying, present in their bodies but backsliding in their hearts, and today their souls had been refreshed and restored. They thanked him because they had been wondering how to witness to their friends at work, and now had better ideas of ways to witness—things to say. Sam had been wrong. His mother had been right. People do need a refresher course.

In Our Hands

Since day one, the church has used one method to reach out to people more frequently and more successfully than any other. It's the way the gospel was brought to Europe by Paul, and the way it spread throughout the West by the Dominican and Franciscan orders, among others. It was central in the life, worship, and outreach of the Reformation. It was the means by which lives were ignited and entire towns transformed in the great awakenings in this country. Today, it remains the one task, more than any other, that most congregations expect of their pastors. It is the main vehicle for communicating to them and the large community God's grace and peace. I'm talking, of course, about preaching. (https://www.christianitytoday.com/pastors/1990/summer/90l3062.html)

This excerpt taken from *ChristianityToday.com* perfectly articulates the value and necessity of preaching as the most effective means of spreading the gospel. The evangelistic sermon has been a powerful tool in the conversion of saints since the salvation plan was first laid out for those gathered in the crowd in Acts 2. However, regardless of all the souls harvested due to the presentation of an evangelistic sermon, preachers seem to have become reserved in their delivering of specifically evangelistic messages. The necessity of evangelistic sermons in a church congregation where members are already saved, sanctified, and delivered has been brought into question.

That same article from *ChristianityToday.com* lists some of the objections being raised against evangelistic sermons. The main problem brought up most often is that evangelistic sermons don't seem to help believers. The thinking is that since evangelistic sermons focus on unbelievers, and most church congregations are made up of those already full of faith, this type of sermon is not needed on the average Sunday morning. That might be so, but evangelistic sermons are helpful to believers as well for three main reasons:

1. Believers continually meet people who need the Lord. These types of sermons help them understand the ways they can tell people about the Lord most effectively. Listening to a preacher express the gospel message grants church members an example for their own expression of faith.

2. Not all believers are articulate in the expression of their faith. Someone who might not be good at expressing each tenet of the gospel themselves might find it very easy to invite their friends to come to church with them. Once there, if an evangelistic message is preached, then the friend will not only see the gospel message in action during the church service, but hear it plainly described and expressed from the pulpit.

3. Just because people attend church faithfully doesn't mean they have a thriving relationship with the Lord Himself. Regular attendees might be just as in need of hearing the gospel and having an opportunity to respond to it as anyone else.

Now that we've established that an evangelistic message is a vital tool to be utilized in regular church services, how do we go about preaching one?

Have you ever experienced a situation in your life where you watched a close friend or relative create so many problems for themselves, falling into pits that might have been easily avoided that you had to sit back and say to yourself "Well, now at least I know what not to do"? Sometimes knowing what not to do is just as valuable as knowing what to do. That's why I love this list provided by Gavin Adams on the six ways to preach a terrible sermon.

1. Don't connect.
   Take away: Connect
   "Content comes through credibility." The degrees you have and the accolades you have won are not the things which give you a good success rate in preaching. To preach a successful sermon, you don't need

those things—you need to connect with and communicate to the people you are trying to minister to."

Academic achievement or worldly acclaim do not mean anything when it comes to crowd credibility. You might be standing behind the pulpit, but that doesn't mean everyone is listening to you or truly hearing what you have to say, especially if they have had prior unfortunate experiences with preachers or ministers in the past. "If you want to ensure your content is never heard, never connect yourself to the audience. They won't care, because they won't know you care."

2. Don't leverage felt needs.
    Take away: Leverage felt needs
    Nothing on earth is so true as the Bible. All truth comes from it. Endless amounts of wisdom and advice are housed within its pages. People are often lazy—this is just the truth—and self-centered. They don't want to go through all the trouble of finding truth in the Scriptures for themselves, but they do want all truth expressed from the Scripture to apply to them personally. They want to know what you are saying will end up benefiting them in some way.

    Presenting the truth of Scripture before engaging their minds is creating "a solution searching for a problem." First, you must identify the tension so that every truth of Scripture has a tension it resolves. The name for this is "identifying the tension." Ask yourself: "What is the problem that needs a solution, the question that needs an answer, the tension that needs resolution, or the mystery that needs illumination?

    "If you want your sermon to be ineffective, be sure to leave out any tension to hear the truth. The Christians will listen politely. The non-believers won't come back."

3. Give tons of information.
    Take away: Be concise
    I'm not sure why, but some preachers seem to believe the more information they provide, the deeper their sermon will be. More information is actually far from the thing people need. The world is inundated with more than enough information. Christians, as a group, run the risk of being over-informed yet under-applied.

    "If your sermon goal is loading up information, please find a better goal. Or, just accept 'ineffective' as your result."

4. Make it boring.

    Take away: Be creative

    People are natural consumers. The church spends a lot of time and energy fighting this mentality, but I propose it as a commodity to be leveraged. If people are visual—give them illustrations. Statistics claim people recall only 10 percent of what they have heard three days after they have heard it. If a picture is added, however, the average recollection rate bumps up to 65 percent.

    Don't fight a statistic like that, sitting around wishing things were different or whining about how people need to be better. Use it to your advantage. Use illustrations to help your congregation leverage info and recall facts. Use catchy statements. Tell colorful stories. Alliterate. Rhyme. Move about. Show video.

    "Of course, you can just read the Bible to them if you prefer. Just make sure to wake them up when it's over."

    It would be amazing if the truth of the Scripture were just soaked up regardless of how interesting or colorful a sermon was. This is not the case, however. Each person possesses God-given creative power. We should be using it.

5. Make it Long.

    Take away: Keep it brief

    No one likes to read a book that has two hundred fifty pages but only one hundred pages of actual content. Authors may repeat themselves over and over to pound in a point, or spend paragraphs crafting unnecessary description. No one likes that, but sometimes sermons can be that way as well.

    "Here's a suggestion: Don't preach the time allotment; preach the time necessary to make your point. Don't preach for time. Preach for purpose."

6. Wing it, or prepare briefly the night before.

    Take away: Plan in advance

    A failure to plan is planning for failure. The time spent preparing a message directly relates to the success of that message. Look ahead. Create series, decide on topics, settle on passages. Don't be rigid. Leave way for the moving of the Spirit, yes, but have a plan.

Myron Augsburger prepares for his sermons by practicing something called "vicarious dialogue." He says:

> As I prepare my sermon, I try to listen to the questions my listeners might have at certain points in my message. Then I craft my sermon to respond to those questions at appropriate points. This forces me to think seriously about the people I'm addressing. It also helps them see that I am not just trying to get them interested in something they don't care about. I'm responding to their interests.
>
> Basically, peruse your own sermon and think to yourself, "What are the loopholes I could possibly find in this material or the questions someone might have about these points?"

When crafting a sermon of any sort, Abram Kielsmeier-Jones recommends reading your text out loud to yourself several times, forming a passage outline, researching the passage, finding and capturing illustrations, and writing an outline or a manuscript.

An outline is more of a point-by-point synopsis of what you will say while a manuscript deals more with the exact wording you will use — a full script if you will. As a speaker, you must decide which will work best for you. Lenny Luchetti recommends literally practicing what you preach by delivering your prepared sermon to an empty room a couple of times.

Larry Moyer points out via preaching.com that an evangelistic message always mentions three truths. "You are a sinner. Christ died for you and arose. You have to trust Christ. Why is that? Because, for a person to come to Christ those are the three things they need to know: They are sinners, Christ died for them and rose the third day, and they need to trust Christ." How do they trust Christ? Through the plan of salvation, three other truths which should always be mentioned in any evangelistic message.

In the Workshop

Have each student in your class prepare a twenty-minute evangelistic sermon using all the pointers contained in the lesson.

Final Inspection

1. Why is evangelistic preaching on the decline?

2. What is the ultimate goal of evangelistic preaching?

3. What are other benefits of evangelistic preaching as stated in this lesson?

4. List ten Bible texts that could be used for an evangelistic sermon.
   A.
   B.
   C.
   D.
   E.
   F.
   G.
   H.
   I.
   J.

5. What three truths should be included in every evangelistic sermon?
   A. _____
   B. _____
   C. _____

6. What does it mean to "connect" with the congregation while preaching an evangelistic sermon?
   _____
   _____
   _____
   _____

7. According to Gavin Adams, what are six ways to craft a positive evangelistic sermon? (What are his "take aways"?)
   A. _____
   B. _____
   C. _____
   D. _____
   E. _____
   F. _____

Personal Study Notes

Lesson 16

Prison Ministry

Project Blueprints

After this lesson, students should be able to

- Be aware of the scriptural admonition to visit those in prison
- Feel the need to minister to those in prison
- Understand the spiritual preparation needed to minister in a prison
- Know how to organize a prison ministry

In the Toolbox

Prison: a building in which people are legally held as punishment for a crime they have committed or while awaiting trial

Prisoner: a person legally held in prison as a punishment for crimes they have committed or while awaiting trial

In His Word

Then the King will say to those on his right, "Come, you who are blessed by my Father; take your inheritance . . . For I was hungry and you gave me something to eat, I was thirsty and you gave me something to drink, I was a stranger and you invited me in, I needed clothes and you clothed me, I was sick and you looked after me, I was in prison and you came to visit me."

Then the righteous will answer him, "Lord, when did we see you hungry and feed you, or thirsty and give you something to drink? When did we see you a stranger and invite you in, or needing clothes and clothe you? When did we see you sick or in prison and go to visit you?'"

The King will reply, "Truly I tell you, whatever you did for one of the least of these brothers and sisters of mine, you did for me." (Matthew 25:34–40, NIV)

Keep on loving each other as Christian brothers. Do not forget to be kind to strangers and let them stay in your home. Some people have had angels in their homes without knowing it. Remember those in prison. Think of them as if you were in prison with them. Remember those who are suffering because of what others have done to them. You may suffer in the same way. (Hebrews 13:1–3, NLV)

In Their Shoes

Tommy was not looking forward to visiting his dad in prison. His father was a cruel and harsh man. Tommy had lived in fear of him while he was still living at home. His dad was loud. He was angry. He would hit them. Both Tommy and his sweet mother had suffered at the hands of his father before a convenience store robbery had finally landed him in prison.

He'd been in prison for almost three years now. This would be the third Christmas Tommy would spend looking at his father on the other side of the glass. He hated coming to the prison more than anything. Hated coming to see his father and having to look in his cold, unfeeling eyes. Hated sitting on the other side of the glass not being good enough—never good enough for his father. He had resigned himself to never feeling his father's love, knowing he was proud, or connecting with him on any level. All that man cared about was himself. He never asked Tommy any personal questions about his life or how he was. He would just spew angry, bitter words as Tommy sat in silence on the other side of the glass.

The door opened in the side of the room and Tommy knew the moment of reckoning had come. He steeled himself for another gruff, awkward encounter. The only reason he was even there was his mother made him visit. She was always loving people when they didn't deserve it and offering forgiveness for unforgivable things.

The guard ushered a man into the visiting area and Tommy blinked multiple times trying to take in what he was seeing. The man walking in before him was Tommy's dad in the sense that he looked like his father, but something was so different about his countenance that Tommy was compelled to study it more closely than ever before. His dad sat down on one side of the glass, picked up the phone used for communication, looked into Tommy's eyes with compassion and love, and said softly, "Hey, kid. How ya doing?"

Tommy's father had not asked him how he was in years. As the conversation went on, he struggled with disbelief at what was occurring. This man in front of him was contrite, compassionate, thoughtful, and funny. Through the course of the conversation, Tommy learned prison evangelists had visited his father, and because the woman who came reminded him so much of Tommy's mother with her long hair and soft eyes, he had listened and come to the Lord at long last. Someone had reached past hope into prison bars and handed Tommy's father, and Tommy himself, a whole new way of life.

In Our Hands

Prisoners are outcasts of society. Bound in chains, kept behind bars, the people who wind up in jail are the last people you want to invite to your home for a holiday party. They have spent their life strung out on drugs, or drunk with wine, beating wives, murdering innocents, stealing from those they share the community with. They kill and destroy, rape and plunder. They aren't usually considerate folks looking toward the needs of others.

Prisoners are frightening. They are worn and weary, hardened by life, tattooed and tainted. Were you to stand next to one of them on the street, you might cross over to the other side. Nothing about their demeanor is as scary as the look of hopelessness in their eyes. Even the well-mannered or innocent of this group carry with them some stigma of shame and wariness.

What if they *did* do it? No. These are not people we want to have our children around, and yet these are exactly the kind of people Jesus came to earth for. His message, His heart, His kingdom are all for the prisoners among us. "It is not the healthy who need a doctor, but the sick. I have not come to call the righteous, but sinners" (Mark 2:17, NIV).

Scripture makes it incredibly clear. Jesus' mission—and ours as well—is to announce to those in bondage that there is hope. Sins can be forgiven. Heads can be lifted. They can finally be free.

> He upholds the cause of the oppressed and gives food to the hungry. The LORD sets prisoners free, the LORD gives sight to the blind, the LORD lifts up those who are bowed down, the LORD loves the righteous. The LORD watches over the foreigner and sustains the fatherless and the widow, but he frustrates the ways of the wicked. (Psalm 146:7-9, NIV)

> I, the LORD, have called you in righteousness; I will take hold of your hand. I will keep you and will make you to be a covenant for the people and a light for the Gentiles, to open eyes that are blind, to free captives from prison and to release from the dungeon those who sit in darkness. (Isaiah 42:6-7, NIV)

> The Spirit of the Sovereign LORD is on me, because the LORD has anointed me to proclaim good news to the poor. He has sent me to bind up the brokenhearted, to proclaim freedom for the captives and release from darkness for the prisoners, to proclaim the year of the LORD's favor and the day of vengeance of our God, to comfort all who mourn, and provide for those who grieve in Zion—to bestow on them a crown of beauty instead of ashes, the oil of joy instead of mourning, and a garment of praise instead of a spirit of despair. They will be called oaks of righteousness, a planting of the LORD for the display of his splendor. (Isaiah 61:1-3, NIV)

> The scroll of the prophet Isaiah was handed to him [Jesus]. Unrolling it, he found the place where it is written: "The Spirit of the Lord is on me, because he has anointed me to preach good news to the poor. He has sent me to proclaim freedom for the prisoners and recovery

of sight for the blind, to set the oppressed free, to proclaim the year of the Lord's favor." (Luke 4:17-19, NIV)

Jesus replied, "**Very truly I tell you**, everyone who sins is a slave to sin. Now a slave has no permanent place in the family, but a son belongs to it forever. So if the Son sets you free, you will be free indeed." (John 8:34-36, NIV)

Jesus spent much time associating with those whom society would otherwise overlook. Prisoners were important to Him, the textbook definition of the exact people He valued and came to save. His love toward the outcasts of society is portrayed beautifully in His exchange with the thief on the cross.

But the other criminal rebuked him. "Don't you fear God," he said, "since you are under the same sentence? We are punished justly, for we are getting what our deeds deserve. But this man has done nothing wrong." Then he said, "Jesus, remember me when you come into your kingdom." Jesus answered him, "Truly I tell you, today you will be with me in paradise." (Luke 23:40-43, NIV)

Here Jesus was hanging on a cross next to someone who had done wrong, and who, unlike our Savior, deserved to be punished. Instead of judging the thief or speaking harshly to him, Jesus expressed love and compassion. The state of mind of our Savior toward prisoners was such that even if the crowd had not chosen to exchange Him for Barabbas that day, Jesus would have died for him. That's what He came for.

A physical prison is not the only sort of trap a man can fall into. We all have sinned. We all have fallen short of the glory of God. (Romans 3:23) We all have experienced bondage in deep darkness, but the Lord has come to deliver and to set us free. Every human soul longs for freedom, even in the midst of captivity.

Maya Angelou knew this, and she wrote about it in her poem on why the caged bird sings:

But a caged BIRD stands on the grave of dreams
His shadow shouts on a nightmare scream
His wings are clipped and his feet are tied

So he opens his throat to sing.

> The caged bird sings with
> A fearful trill of things unknown
> But longed for still and his
> Tune is heard on the distant hill
> For the caged bird sings of freedom.

Even a caged bird understands there is a freedom that can be found behind steel bars. After all, where the Spirit of the Lord is there is freedom (II Corinthians 3:17). Where two or three are gathered in His name, He will be in the midst of them (Matthew 18:20). So you can walk right into a prison to meet with prisoners — the kind of people Jesus really loved — and share the light of His Word, and His presence will be right there. It surely showed up in a tangible way in a prison in Acts 16.

> About midnight Paul and Silas were praying and singing hymns to God, and the other prisoners were listening to them. Suddenly there was such a violent earthquake that the foundations of the prison were shaken. At once all the prison doors flew open, and everyone's chains came loose. (Acts 16:25-26, NIV)

What if you looked beyond fear, nerves, and prejudice to the see the people God loves? This could be said of the work God does through your ministry:

> Some sat in darkness and deepest gloom, imprisoned in iron chains of misery. They rebelled against the words of God, scorning the counsel of the Most High. That is why he broke them with hard labor, they fell, and no one was there to help them. "LORD, help!" they cried in their trouble, and he saved them from their distress. He led them from the darkness and deepest gloom; he snapped their chains. Let them praise the LORD for his great love and for the wonderful things he has done for them. For he broke down their prison gates of bronze; he cut apart their bars of iron. (Psalm 107:10-16, NLT)

In the Workshop

Encourage your class to visit a local prison and develop a plan for ministry there. Who can they contact about the possibility? What would the warden allow or not allow? Can they set up a system to minister to those recently released from prison as well?

Final Inspection

1. Cite five scriptural references to prisoners.
   A. _____
   B. _____
   C. _____
   D. _____
   E. _____

2. How would you prepare spiritually, mentally, and emotionally to minister in a prison?
   _____
   _____
   _____
   _____

3. What physical or material needs might a prisoner have that you could meet?
   _____
   _____
   _____
   _____

4. How would you begin to organize a prison ministry?
   _____
   _____
   _____
   _____

5. What would be your follow-up plan for those released from prison?

Lesson 17

Reaching the Elderly

Project Blueprints

After this lesson, students should be able to

- Respect the elderly as a biblical mandate
- Value the elderly for what they have to contribute to the church and community
- Devise ways of helping the aged physically, emotionally, and mentally
- Plan ways of ministering spiritually to the aged
- Establish a ministry to the residents of a local retirement or nursing home

In the Toolbox

Elderly: of a person old or aging

In His Word

Do not rebuke an older man but encourage him as you would a father, younger men as brothers. (I Timothy 5:1, ESV)

You shall stand up before the gray head and honor the face of an old man, and you shall fear your God: I am the LORD. (Leviticus 19:32, ESV)

Do not cast me off in the time of old age; forsake me not when my strength is spent. (Psalm 71:9, ESV)

Let the elders who rule well be considered worthy of double honor, especially those who labor in preaching and teaching. (I Timothy 5:17, ESV)

Even to your old age I am he, and to gray hairs I will carry you. I have made, and I will bear; I will carry and will save. (Isaiah 46:4, ESV)

Gray hair is a crown of glory; it is gained in a righteous life. (Proverbs 16:31, ESV)

Wisdom is with the aged, and understanding in length of days. (Job 12:12, ESV)

So I exhort the elders among you, as a fellow elder and a witness of the sufferings of Christ, as well as a partaker in the glory that is going to be revealed. (I Peter 5:1, ESV)

Likewise, you who are younger, be subject to the elders. Clothe yourselves, all of you, with humility toward one another, for "God opposes the proud but gives grace to the humble." (I Peter 5:5, ESV)

In Their Shoes

Bertha sat alone staring out the window. That seemed to be her favorite pastime these days. The Lord knew she hadn't had much else to do for four years. That's how long she had been living at the retirement home.

It had taken some convincing to get Bertha to make the move; the virtues of the home had been loudly expounded in her hearing: She would have twenty-four-hour care. She would be around people her own age. She would benefit from all the extracurricular activities the home provided and receive medical attention quickly whenever she needed it. Most of all, her children would come and visit her at least once a week.

They did that for about a month. It had now been eight months since she had seen any of her children and grandchildren. She already knew they would not be coming over the holidays, because they were taking a huge family vacation to Key West, Florida.

She had resigned herself to her fate months ago. She would die here alone in this home, and no one would notice she was gone or miss her. How she longed to know that someone somewhere cared about her. How she longed to have a close relationship with someone once again. If only someone would introduce her to a friend who would understand and stay with her.

No sooner had she thought this than a knock sounded at her door. When she gave permission for the door to be opened, a young man holding a Bible stepped into the room. That was the moment Bertha met David, a friend in the flesh who would care for her and visit her regularly until her death. But more importantly, David was the man who introduced her to Jesus, and after that day Bertha was never alone again.

In Our Hands

Different cultures react in different ways when it comes to the elderly. In America, for example, those who are aging seem to lack respect. Anthropologist Jared Diamond, who has spent years observing and tracking the attitude younger people have toward their elders across the world, says, "In countries like the UK and the US the elderly live lonely lives separated from their children and their lifelong friends." He notes as the health of people declines in these cultures, they are often moved to homes or retirement communities—places where they will receive care and assisted living by someone who is paid to look after them.

China stands in stark contrast to this culture in America; looking after and revering one's parents is a governmental statute there. Elderly parents can saddle their children with a lawsuit if they are not receiving enough support—both emotional and financial.

Theweek.com points out that France also protects parents by law. The Elderly Rights Law was passed in 2004 in Article 207 of the Civil Code. This law requires citizens to keep in touch with their geriatric parents. The article points out, however, that unlike China, this law does not take root in respect. It was enacted after a publication of statistics revealed France as having the highest rate of pensioner suicides on the European continent. It came into play following a heat wave that killed 15,000 people. The majority of those killed were elderly, and they had been deceased for several weeks before they were looked for or found.

Social Gerontology: A Multidisciplinary Perspective informs us that the culture of respecting elders is high in Japan, where many generations live under one roof. The Japanese administration on aging states that more people over the age of sixty-five are in the country than any other group, adding that 7.2 percent of Japanese people will be over eighty by the year 2020.

Aplaceformom.com lets us know Scotland has a new program called Reshaping Care for Older People that its citizens are required to obey. Mediterranean and people of Latin ethnicity are generally looked upon as "one big happy family."

A study in *American Ethnologist* shows the Chuckchi of Siberia practice voluntary death. This means that an old person commonly requests to die at the hand of a close relative when they are no longer in good health. *The World Since Yesterday* also touches on the habit of this practice, explaining how the Crow Indians in the US as well as Norse tribes in Scandinavia oftentimes put themselves in precarious and impossible situations like setting sail on a solo voyage they are not likely to survive. That study also communicated how the Aché of Paraguay let their men roam off to die alone on "the white man's road" while the tribe kills elderly women by breaking their necks.

It's not all gloom and doom, however. *The New York Times* reported once that the Greek Island of Ikaria is seemingly magical in its life-extending power. People who live on this tiny island in the Mediterranean Sea are four times more likely to live to ninety than those in America. They also live an extra eight to ten years longer on average after being diagnosed with cancer or heart defects. What's their secret? They linger. They enjoy life. They don't scurry or hurry. They stay up late enjoying the fruits of their island, swimming in the water, and amusing themselves as they drink mountain tea. More likely than not, the eating patterns and relaxed style of its people account for some of the longevity of its people, but there is no set explanation for the way most of the population manages to live so well so long.

In Ghana where I grew up, respect for elders was imperative. I still remember my friend Sophia telling me how when someone talked back to an elder in their village, the disrespectful person would be placed in a deep hole in the ground, buried up to his or her neck, and left to the woods and the fire ants. I'm not sure how factual this story was, or how great a disrespect discrepancy would need to be committed to merit such treatment, but after that I thought twice before snapping back to an elder.

As Christians, we believe that all human beings deserve respect and proper treatment. We are to love people as the Lord loves them, as if we are loving the Lord Himself. Beyond that, what does the Bible say specifically about the elderly? We are definitely admonished to obey our parents in the Lord, for this is right (Ephesians 6:1).

Even as Jesus hung on the cross, He was worried about His mother.

> When Jesus therefore saw his mother, and the disciple standing by, whom he loved, he saith unto his mother, Woman, behold thy son! Then saith he to the disciple, Behold thy mother! And from that hour that disciples took her unto his own home. (John 19:26-27)

Hanging on a cross, carrying the literal weight of the world on His shoulders, Jesus was worried about His mother being well taken care of. At the end of His life, some of His final thoughts were about an elderly woman. An elderly woman was one of the first people He encountered at the beginning of His life as well.

> And there was a prophetess, Anna, the daughter of Phanuel, of the tribe of Asher. She was advanced in years, having lived with her husband seven years from when she was a virgin, and then as a widow until she was eighty-four. She did not depart from the temple, worshiping with fasting and prayer night and day. And

coming up at that very hour she began to give thanks to God and to speak of him to all who were waiting for the redemption of Jerusalem. (Luke 2:36-38, ESV)

God revered elderly people so much that they were some of the first to know Messiah had finally come and they recognized Him for who He truly was.

And, behold, there was a man in Jerusalem, whose name was Simeon; and the same man was just and devout, waiting for the consolation of Israel: and the Holy Ghost was upon him. And it was revealed unto him by the Holy Ghost, that he should not see death, before he had seen the Lord's Christ. And he came by the Spirit into the temple: and when the parents brought in the child Jesus, to do for him after the custom of the law, then took he him up in his arms, and blessed God, and said, Lord, now lettest thou thy servant depart in peace, according to thy word: for mine eyes have seen thy salvation, which thou hast prepared before the face of all people; a light to lighten the Gentiles, and the glory of thy people Israel. And Joseph and his mother marvelled at those things which were spoken of him. (Luke 2:25-33)

Elders are revered and spoken well of throughout the Bible. I especially love these beautiful words spoken of Moses: "Moses was one hundred and twenty years old when he died. His eye was undimmed, and his vigor unabated." (Deuteronomy 34:7, ESV)

Not only are we to revere and help elders, but elders are a help to us in ways only they can be. "Remember the days of old; consider the generations long past. Ask your father and he will tell you, your elders, and they will explain to you" (Deuteronomy 32:7, NIV).

Any person can technically care for the elderly, but the elderly provide us with something we cannot get anywhere else: wisdom and life experience. They know the way of the Lord, having walked in it for a long time, and have seen firsthand the miracles He has performed.

The elderly are a valuable asset to our walk of faith and our communities. Religionnews.com calls evangelizing to elders "preaching at the last bus stop to eternity." A volunteer named Lauren Bowerfind, who evangelizes in nursing homes, states, "Many of these people don't have friends or families that visit. We're the only Jesus they may see."

Whatever the culture of your country, whoever the elderly people you have in your own home and family, the Lord loves them and it is His will for them to know they are wanted and valued in His kingdom. During the time in their lives when the gospel message might be the last they receive, we are called to speak it to them loudly and clearly.

In the Workshop

Discuss with your students the elderly people who might be present in their lives. What have they done to notice, witness to, or better the lives of those people? What else can they do to make sure they receive the gospel and hear of God's love?

Final Inspection

1. Why do you think Americans and the British tend to devalue the elderly?

   _____
   _____
   _____
   _____
   _____

2. What roles have your grandparents played in your life?

   _____
   _____
   _____
   _____
   _____

3. What can the elderly contribute to the local congregation?

   _____
   _____
   _____
   _____

4. Your neighbor is a widow without any family nearby. List five things you can do to help her.
   A. _____
   B. _____
   C. _____
   D. _____
   E. _____

5. List five things to consider when planning a nursing home service.
   A. _____
   B. _____
   C. _____
   D. _____
   E. _____

Lesson 18

Door Knocking

Project Blueprints

After this lesson, students should be able to

- Discuss the pros and cons of door-to-door evangelism
- Recognize physical hindrances to door-to-door evangelism
- Design material for door-to-door evangelism
- Consider more effective means of evangelism other than going door to door

In the Toolbox

Door knocking: To go to each house or apartment in an area to talk with the people who live there. Example: "Political campaign workers have been knocking on doors throughout the neighborhood."

In His Word

Neither do people light a lamp and put it under a bowl. Instead they put it on its stand, and it gives light to everyone in the house. In the same way, let your light shine before others, that they may see your good deeds and glorify your Father in heaven. (Matthew 5:15–16, NIV)

Therefore go and make disciples of all nations, baptizing them in the name of the Father and of the Son and of the Holy Spirit, and teaching them to obey everything I have commanded you. And surely I am with you always, to the very end of the age. (Matthew 28:19-20, NIV)

This is to my Father's glory, that you bear much fruit, showing yourselves to be my disciples. (John 15:8, NIV)

But you will receive power when the Holy Spirit comes on you; and you will be my witnesses in Jerusalem, and in all Judea and Samaria, and to the ends of the earth. (Acts 1:8, NIV)

But not all the Israelites accepted the good news. For Isaiah says, "Lord, who has believed our message?" Consequently, faith comes from hearing the message, and the message is heard through the word about Christ. (Romans 10:16-17, NIV)

We are therefore Christ's ambassadors, as though God were making His appeal through us. We implore you on Christ's behalf: Be reconciled to God. (II Corinthians 5:20, NIV)

On the contrary, they recognized that I had been entrusted with the task of preaching the gospel to the uncircumcised, just as Peter had been to the circumcised. For God, who was at work in Peter as an apostle to the circumcised, was also at work in me as an apostle to the Gentiles. James, Cephas and John, those esteemed as pillars, gave me and Barnabas the right hand of fellowship when they recognized the grace given to me. They agreed that we should go to the Gentiles, and they to the circumcised. (Galatians 2:7-9, NIV)

In Their Shoes

Kathy felt door knocking was cringy. She was an introvert, living to help, improve, and create happiness in the lives of others. Showing up at someone's door unannounced to infringe upon his or her day was way out of her comfort zone.

The church, however, was doing an outreach today. Her pastor had made such a good case for warning souls about the imminent danger they were in and pulling them back from the brink of Hell that Kathy knew she could not stay home and do homework that Saturday. As much as she hated it, she was going to have to participate in going door to door.

She wasn't sure this was the most effective form of evangelism, but she was submitted to her pastor and committed to the cause of Christ. She trusted the Lord, believed in His Word, and knew He would multiply her efforts. She sighed, stilled her beating heart, sent one last plea for help heavenward, and knocked on the door in front of her.

A young woman about her age opened the door. "Can I help you?" she asked.

"Yes," Kathy half stuttered, "I'm sorry to interrupt your day, but my church is going around visiting members of the community and asking if there's anything we can help people pray about."

The woman in front of Kathy immediately burst into tears. Kathy wasn't sure what she had done wrong. To be honest, she had expected things to go badly, but not this badly. When the woman was finally able to choke out her story, Kathy learned she had been on the verge of taking her own life that day and had prayed to God one last time. "If You really care about me," she had prayed, "You will send someone to my door right now."

In Our Hands

Door-to-door evangelism, otherwise known as "canvassing," is often looked upon with disdain. Showing up at someone's house uninvited might not be the ideal way to insert yourself into their good opinion. I personally do not like to be infringed upon or interrupted as I go about my day or dinner with my family all so a stranger can try to "sell" me the latest fad they have bought into.

There is no biblical mandate to evangelize by going door to door — although Jesus did say that He "stands at the door and knocks" (Revelation 3:20). In fact, the Scripture says:

> Carry no money belt, no bag, no shoes; and greet no one on the way. Whatever house you enter, first say, "Peace be to this house." If a man of peace is there, your peace will rest on him; but if not, it will return to you. Stay in that house, eating and drinking what they give you; for the laborer is worthy of his wages. Do not keep moving from house to house. (Luke 10:4–7, NASB)

No record exists of the Christians in the early church going from door to door. We know they taught the Word in the Temple every day (Acts 2:46) and spoke about the Lord in the homes of those in the church whenever they could (Acts 5:42). Paul and other missionaries, and ministers like him, witnessed often to those in the village market (Acts 17:17). No record occurs, however, of the early Christians walking door to door, canvassing their neighborhoods.

While no explicit mandate for this particular method of evangelism is recorded, we are instructed to share our faith with everyone we can, whenever we can. We are to have the ability or to be prepared to speak about the Lord and His love at any given moment.

If no specific biblical mandate exists in favor of door-to-door evangelism—why do it? What are the pros to engaging in that endeavor?

Jehovah's Witnesses often come to mind when discussing this topic. Every member of the church, whether they have been baptized, is required to participate in the work of door-to-door evangelism. Those who journey door to door witnessing are called "publishers." They are expected to return with a full report of their activity, including how many hours of their month they spent going door-to-door witnessing and how many of those experiences culminated in the delivering of a further Bible story to willing parties.

That is their policy, but how effective is it? Gotquestions.org informs us that in 2012 the Jehovah's Witnesses group had 7.5 million "publishers." They saw over 260,000 people baptized in their organization. This means that on average, 6,500 hours' worth of activity culminates in one baptism.

Statistically speaking, door-to-door evangelism is not the most effective form, but does that mean it's not worth the effort? Is one soul not worth 6,500 hours to the Lord, for example?

Arguably, if you knew your city would soon be set on fire or destroyed by an atomic bomb, you would likely be the first person to run throughout the streets, pounding on doors, yelling at the top of your lungs in order to warn innocent people of the impending danger they were soon to face. If we truly believe people are standing on the precipice of Hell, we should be eager to warn them of their certain fate.

Both pros and cons exist for door-to-door evangelism. All evangelism should follow the principles listed in this verse: "But in your hearts honor Christ the Lord as holy, always being prepared to make a defense to anyone who asks you for a reason for the hope that is in you; yet do it with gentleness and respect" (I Peter 3:15, ESV).

Are you honoring Christ with your method of evangelism? Are you prepared to make a defense to anyone who asks you about the hope in you, and share that hope with others? Are you practicing evangelism with gentleness and respect for others? These are the most important questions to ask.

If you choose to embark on the journey of door-to-door evangelism, some important tips to keep in mind are derived from an article on the website whatchristiansneedtoknow.com:

1. **Respect their privacy.**
   Refrain from peering through windows or opening doors uninvited. If there is a doorbell, use it. If no doorbell is present, knock on the door quickly and precisely.

2. **Do not linger.**
   If no one comes to the door within a minute, then leave whatever witnessing materials you have with you at the door. Some important things to include in witnessing materials would be the plan of salvation, and your church information (phone number, address, website, etc.).

3. **Consider their property.**
   Don't stroll across someone's yard, trample over their gardens, or climb or throw things over their gates.

4. **Check for animals.**
   If there are guard signs posted or vicious dogs chained to fences, avoid the property. Evangelism is important, but so is your safety.

5. **Avoid interacting with children.**
   If a person's offspring are playing around their house, feel free to nod or wave at them but never speak to them before speaking to their parents. Remember if the children were yours, you might not appreciate strangers engaging them in conversation without your presence.

6. **Apologize.**
   A well-phrased apology is a perfect way to show your consideration for invading someone's space and taking her time. Ask if you or your church can do anything for the individual or the community, or if you can help her pray about a need.

7. **Be aware of the time.**
   This is meant in two ways:

   First, be aware of the time you are arriving at someone's house. Dinner time might be an inconvenient moment to show up, as well as early in the morning when they are leaving for work or late at night when they might already be in bed. The same time might not work for different families or different neighborhoods. Some trial and error might need to be employed.

   Second, be aware of how much time you are spending speaking to the person about the Lord. You want to stay on topic, communicate as clearly as possible, and avoid boring the individual or overstaying your welcome.

8. **Take a companion with you.**
   You never know what situations or people you might encounter when canvassing door to door. It is wise to take a companion with you. Make sure, however, that the companions you choose are appropriate ones. You will not want to put a single person with a married person of the opposite sex, for example. Mixed groups (unless the people are married to each other) should travel in groups of three.

   The ultimate goal is not to bump up numbers for church attendance, or to see how many houses you can visit, but to share the good news of

Jesus Christ with as many people as possible, in the most effective manner possible.

In the Workshop

Discuss with your class whether outreach or evangelistic material is available for a door-knocking endeavor in your area. If no material is available, work with the class on creating a pamphlet or a flier with the full plan of salvation and local church information. If material is already available in your area, dedicate a portion of your class time to getting out on the streets and intentionally sharing the good news with the people in homes around your school.

Final Inspection

1. List five reasons to evangelize door to door.
   A. _____
   B. _____
   C. _____
   D. _____
   E. _____

2. List five arguments against evangelizing door to door.
   A. _____
   B. _____
   C. _____
   D. _____
   E. _____

3. What should be included in material for door-to-door evangelism?
   _____
   _____
   _____
   _____

4. You live next to a high-rise apartment complex that has tight security. What methods of evangelism would you use to reach the residents?

   _____
   _____
   _____
   _____

5. In going door to door, list five tips that you should follow.
   A. _____
   B. _____
   C. _____
   D. _____
   E. _____

6. You have designed material for door-to-door evangelism. List five other methods of evangelism that could use the pamphlet or flyer.
   A. _____
   B. _____
   C. _____
   D. _____
   E. _____

Lesson 19

Cell Groups

Project Blueprints

After this lesson, students should be able to

- Understand the mechanics of a cell group
- Discern the purpose of a cell group
- Recognize various types of cell groups
- Know how to start a cell group

In the Toolbox

Cell groups: A form of church organization that is used in many Christian churches. Cell groups are generally intended to teach the Bible and personalize Christian fellowship.

Cell groups: Nurturing groups of 8–12 where regular worship, intercessory prayer, accountability, and fellowship around God's Word binds the individuals into a cohesive unit. Here these individuals can use their spiritual gifts, receive support, encourage each other, and seek to bring others to share their joy. (foundationsforfreedom.net)

Cell groups: "Groups of three to fifteen people who meet weekly outside the church building for the purpose of evangelism, community, and spiritual growth with the goal of multiplication." —Joel Comiskey

In His Word

> And they, continuing daily with one accord in the temple, and breaking bread from house to house, did eat their meat with gladness and singleness of heart. (Acts 2:46)

In Their Shoes

Meg had promised herself and everyone she knew she would never darken the doors of a church. Religion was for idiots who needed something to appease their conscience, to help them sleep at night. Meg had no problem with her conscience; she was used to drowning out its incessant nagging. Religion was for people who cared about their lives and what happened to them. Meg didn't care about any of that. Not anymore, seeing how she ended up.

She was pretty sure she didn't deserve happiness anyway. No, Meg would not darken the doors of a church. She didn't need religion, and religion certainly didn't want her. She would never confess to a priest, never speak to a preacher. She did, however, work a job at a local restaurant, and she would certainly speak to the people involved. It was at her job that Meg met Bianca.

Bianca was a religious person, but Meg didn't even notice for a couple of weeks. Sure, Bianca dressed differently, always wearing skirts, but she never made Meg feel guilty, weird, or judged. She was just who she was—loving, nice, friendly—and she accepted Meg for who she was too. Meg had never felt so loved as she did in Bianca's presence. When Bianca invited Meg to church, she reacted differently than any other time she had received such an invitation. Sure, she still said no. She was committed to never darkening church doors.

However, she said no with a little less venom. She almost wanted to go. Bianca was so loving, such a light and delight to be around. Meg had a hard time imagining anything Bianca did or believed in being wrong, harsh, or judgmental. She stood her ground through multiple invitations. Still, Meg wouldn't go to church. But she would go to Bianca's house for dessert.

And that is how she found herself a member of the cell group that met in Bianca's home. When Meg would not go to church, she encountered God in Bianca and church body in her in living room. The truth she heard at that cell group changed her whole life. Now, she goes to church every Sunday. The church where she has found a home. The church where Bianca baptized her in Jesus' name.

In Our Hands

The names have changed, but the above story happens to be true. Not only is it true, but it took place in the cell group I attend at my local church, in the home of my good friend "Bianca." "Bianca" had endured a lot of hardship in her life that few would understand. When everything was going wrong, the church hadn't made much room for her. Because of this, she had a great burden for making sure her home had room for everyone, a seat for everyone at her table. The gift of hospitality is thriving within her spirit, but even if it weren't, it would be her responsibility to shelter and shepherd others to Christ. It is a responsibility all of us carry.

> As you come to him, the living Stone—rejected by humans but chosen by God and precious to Him—you also, like living stones, are being built into a spiritual house to be a holy priesthood, offering spiritual sacrifices acceptable to God through Jesus Christ. (I Peter 2:4-5, NIV)

We do not just attend church. We are the church. We are meant to go outside of the four walls of our church buildings, living "bricks" that are an extension of the work of God in the world. A cell group is the perfect way to practice this in our daily lives.

> The purpose of a cell group is to create a Christian fellowship with one another and God that lives among the non-Christian community; to let the Light of Christ shine through each member in order to touch the lives of those around them; to bring them to the feet of Jesus and the fellowship of His body, the church; and to teach them to walk in His steps. —David Finnell

What does a cell group look like? What are some of the basic building blocks of cell group structure? Foundationsforfreedom.net offers some clarification:

1. Cell groups meet regularly. (And I would add—often.)
2. Spiritual growth (both of members and leaders) is the fundamental purpose.
3. Community: a genuine sense of connection formed through the intimacy of a smaller group
4. Penetration evangelism: Reaching out into the community or neighborhood is an intentional aspect of the cell group ministry. It exists for the purpose of spiritual growth, yes, but also reaching out.
5. Multiplication is expected. "When a group grows (through evangelism) it is anticipated that, like every healthy cell, it will multiply." —Mark Howell

Every cell group meets the above qualifications and has the same basic structure, but not all cell groups are created equal, nor are they the same. Many different types of cell groups exist:

1. Open Cell Group
   Motto: The more the merrier.
   Come on in! Anyone can join at any time for any reason. Focused on openness and outreach, there is less chance to grow closer to each other in an intimate way that builds trust because the group is always evolving, but everyone is always welcome. A downside to this would be the casual feel invoking less commitment from everyone involved.

2. Closed Cell Group:
   Motto: Us four and no more
   Not just anyone can waltz in off the street and become a part of this group. There will be a start date after which new people are not welcome to join, and the group will close. During the time it is closed, one topic of study is likely to be focused on until the topic has been covered and the group opens again to accept more members. A high level of closeness is a benefit to a group like this, but it also leads to exclusiveness and clique culture.

3. Free-Market Cell Group
   Motto: Welcome to the club!

This kind of group involves people with common interests meeting together outside of the church to practice their hobbies as they grow in the Lord. Members meet and practice interests they have in common and learn more about the Lord and each other as they do.

4. Neighborhood Cell Groups
   Motto: Could you be mine, would you be mine, won't you be my neighbor?
   This type of small group is portioned out by geography. It limits membership to those within a certain quadrant of physical space, choosing members based on a map. It does really allow members to connect and do life together while cutting down on commute time. The disadvantages are restrictive membership options.

5. Sermon-based Cell Group
   Motto: Sing them over again to me, wonderful words of life.
   This group will review the sermon preached on Sunday while digging deeper into the thoughts and text the pastor presented. It encourages the implementation of the Word in daily life but does not offer a lot of flexibility.

Mark Howell gives us three important things to remember concerning cell groups:

1. Every small group model, system or strategy, will come with a unique set of advantages and disadvantages.
2. The model you choose should be predetermined by what you hope to accomplish.
3. You should choose your model carefully, and only change it after much careful consideration.

Whatever cell group model you choose, keep in mind the three main points and purposes of a cell group.

1. Evangelism and nurturing
2. Pastoral care

3. Leadership development (Naomi Dowdy—*Ministry Today* magazine)

Cell groups are not a modern idea. In fact, they were prominent in the Book of Acts as believers faced persecution. Actually, when Emperor Constantine put an end to the persecution of Christians and the God's people began building church buildings in AD 323, the church numbers actually showed a marked decline. The Book of Acts cells were beyond mere prayer groups or times of fellowship. They were church-like structures where the Word was imparted and the Spirit moved in people's homes. A Book of Acts church implements the use of cell groups. A Book of Acts church fosters community and operates in love. A Book of Acts church turns the world upside down.

In the Workshop

Discuss with your class the following questions and answers taken from Peter M. Senge (*The Fifth Discipline*, New York: Doubleday, 1990) and then help them work through a mock plan for starting a cell group in their local community.

1. What is my first step?
   Discover the cell group vision.
2. How do I get people on board with the vision?
   Develop vision and strategy as a team.
3. Will cell groups work in my church?
   Assess your church's current reality.
4. How do we prepare the church for cell group success?
   Prepare the church through transformation.
5. How do we start the first groups?
   Launch the first groups with kingdom-seekers.
6. How do we experience dynamic cell group community and not just cell group meetings?
   Generate cell group momentum.
7. How do we establish cell groups as the base of the church?
   Establish the hidden systems that support the cells.
8. How we mobilize groups to reach people?
   Expand the cell groups to reach the unreached.

Final Inspection

1. In your opinion, since Meg was determined not to go to a church, why did she attend Bianca's cell group?

   _____
   _____
   _____
   _____

2. Describe the cell group you envision for your neighborhood.

   _____
   _____
   _____
   _____
   _____

3. What are the three main goals of a cell group?
   A. _____
   B. _____
   C. _____

4. List three different types of cell groups.
   A. _____
   B. _____
   C. _____

5. List three things to consider when thinking about starting a cell group.
   A. _____
   B. _____
   C. _____

Missionary Spotlight
Ray and Judi Nicholls

The before-and after-photos of Ray and Judi Nicholls are amazing. He was a pot-smoking soldier when his buddy introduced him to his sister Judi, a hard-drinking marine. Today Ray Nicholls is a self-sacrificing, visionary, pioneering missionary in several of the former Soviet Union republics. His wife's genuine compassion and spiritual sensitivity greatly complement her husband's ministry.

Ray and Judi Nicholls received the Holy Ghost and were baptized in Jesus' name in 1975 in Eau Claire, Wisconsin. In 1978, he left his job in computer technology to become the principal of New Hope Christian School, a ministry of Pentecostal Assembly of Eau Claire. In 1989, he added a Bachelor of Science in Marketing Education to his degree in computer science. In the years that followed, Governor Tommy Thompson appointed him to a four-year term on the Wisconsin State Education Committee. Nicholls also served a two-year term as the vice president of Eau Claire's City Council.

In 1992, Nicholls received a phone call, inviting him to be the coordinator for the School of Tomorrow in Belarus. Like Aquila and Priscilla in the Book of Acts, he and his wife and son Nathan walked through the open door. He became the president and founder of New Hope Christian Schools in Belarus, establishing several Christian schools and directing teacher training—and at one time supervising twenty associates in missions who came to Belarus to teach in Christian schools and to establish Apostolic churches. Thankfully, the new Belarussian government allowed them to conduct church services as they established Accelerated Christian Education schools.

During this time, Nicholls taught in several universities, spoke in public schools in Belarus, and established a church of seventy members in Minsk. (His first convert came from his marketing class at the university.) In addition, he taught, trained, and mentored leaders who are presently serving as pastors in churches throughout Belarus. In 1995, after serving as an AIMer for three years, Ray Nicholls received his ministerial license and a missionary appointment to Belarus.

After grounding the work in Belarus, Ray and Judi Nicholls planted the United Pentecostal Church in Poland, establishing and training national leaders to help shoulder the work, opening churches in six cities.

Presently the Nichollses are appointed to Poland, Belarus, and Ukraine. Along with Mark Shutes, Ray co-founded Revival by Design, a strategy for continued revival and Bible training. Through this effort he has helped to open more than forty-four Bible training centers throughout Europe and the Middle East.

Pastor Sergey Tomev translates for Ray Nicholls in Kiev, Ukraine, November 2015.

Ray Nicholls is also the area coordinator for the nations of the former Soviet Union. He travels extensively throughout this area, leading many to a fuller understanding of the Bible through RBD seminars. And as Europe/Middle East Region's representative on the Global Missions Global Education Committee, he wholeheartedly encourages and furthers the development and advancement of Global Association of Theological Studies and GATS Faculty Advancement Seminars throughout Europe and the Middle East.

Because Ray and Judi Nicholls walked through an open door into ministry, multitudes who were once behind an iron curtain are rejoicing as the Spirit of God is poured out in Eastern Europe and the republics of the former USSR.

Editor's Note: Due to health concerns, Ray and Judi Nicholls retired from full-time missionary involvement in March 2019. Nevertheless, they still conduct seminars and training sessions in Eastern Europe as health, money, and time permit. More recently, the Nicholls agreed to be the interim pastor of their home church in Eau Claire, Wisconsin.